D0828856

Gifts
from Heaven

Gifts from Heaven

Providence in Our Family

Tom and Mary Hartmann

NEW CITY PRESS
Hyde Park, NY

Published in the United States by New City Press
202 Comforter Blvd., Hyde Park, NY 12538
www.newcitypress.com
©2012 Tom and Mary Hartmann

Cover design by Durva Correia

Library of Congress Cataloging-in-Publication Data

Hartmann, Mary.
  Gifts from heaven : providence in our family / Mary and Tom Hartmann.
     p. cm.
  Includes bibliographical references (p.   )
  ISBN 978-1-56548-429-0 (pbk. : alk. paper)
  1. Families--Religious life. 2. Providence and government of
God--Christianity. 3. Christian life--Catholic authors. 4. Hartmann,
Mary--Family. 5. Hartmann, Tom--Family. I. Hartmann, Tom. II. Title.
  BX2351.H367 2012
  231'.5--dc23
                                        2011043075

Printed in the United States of America

*To all our rascals who made us
a family and our best Providence:*

*Tommy, Christina, Peter,
Jennie, Matthew, Maria,
Annamarie, Paul,
Teresa, and Mark*

&

Our twenty grandchildren

&

Those yet to come.

Contents

Preface

Because God loves every person in a particular way, Providence manifests itself in every family. Although some do not recognize it, the Providence of God pours down gifts continuously on all families. We who have faith should find it easier to see the hand of God in the events of our lives, especially those that we cannot explain in any other way. We believe that there is a "golden thread" in each person's life, a pattern of divine gifts that can be perceived when life is examined with the eyes of faith.

Many families, large or small, experience the same things that ours has. We have been helped to become more aware of God's presence in our lives through sharing experiences over many years with other couples who have ideals similar to ours. Together we have learned that whatever happens is permitted or willed by God; everything is God's love for us.

Always being surprised by the gifts of Providence might suggest that we lack faith in God's "steadfast love" — a major theme often repeated in the Book of Psalms: "His steadfast love endures forever." Repeated and beautifully concentrated in Psalm 136, it is also coupled with "and his faithfulness endures forever" (e.g., Ps 117) and "for his wonderful works to humankind" (Ps 107). We need to be full of faith because God is faith-full in his Providence. We should expect his love to be steadfast; we should not be surprised by his Providence, "his wonderful works" on our behalf. We should expect these wonderful works every day because

God's love is "steadfast" and "endures forever." We surely need to have more faith.

Were it strong enough, our faith would let us see Providence working in everything that happens to us, in everything we do, in everything. Is this not the natural and logical result of believing and understanding that God loves each of us immensely?

Ah, but too seldom have we had this kind of strong and consistent faith in Providence. The proof is that again and again we have been surprised by God's gifts. Maybe God gives us so much so often in order to remind us that he is still there, still loving us even when we forget him, even when we go on with our lives as if he does not exist. Too quickly we become distracted by the things we make and do, thinking that we alone control our lives. We forget our Maker. We need a Moses to remind us that we may be worshiping a golden calf.

Introduction

Providence thinks of me much more (indeed very
much more) than I think of it.
I keep it present for a few moments in my day.
It keeps me present all the day long.

IGINO GIORDANI[1]

W hen we got married some forty-five years ago,
in our hearts we felt a strong desire, a calling, to
have a large family. We thought of thirteen as our lucky
number, so why not aim for thirteen children? We were
young and rash and very generous. We both believed
that God would take care of us and our children, no
matter how many he would send us.

We also believed that a human person is the most
precious treasure in creation and that every child is a
unique and divine gift. We understood the great privi-
lege of cooperating with God in bringing such gifts into
the world.

14K Craftsmith

Right from the start Providence gave us a push.
When we figured out our budget for the wedding,
we found that we had enough money to pay only for
Mary's ring, which was elegant but not expensive. We
had nothing left to buy one for Tom. Even though we
had hoped for a double-ring ceremony, we were willing
to settle for one rather than postpone the wedding. So

---

1. *Diary of Fire*, March 9, 1944 (London: New City, 1981), p. 19.

we picked up Mary's ring at Macy's department store a few days before the wedding. When we came outside we were waiting at the traffic light when Tom looked down and saw something shiny at the curb. He picked it up and said, "Hey, Mary, look what I found! A gold ring!" She said, "Try it on! See if it fits!" Sure enough, Tom was able to slip it onto his ring finger with no trouble. "It must have slipped off the finger of some man so old his body was shrinking," Tom said. But Mary was more cautious: "Look inside to see if there is a name in it." Tom took it off, looked inside, and read: " '14K Craftsmith.' Do you think that's someone's name? Or the brand name?" Mary thought it must be a brand and said, "It must have fallen from heaven! I think God wants us both to have rings at our wedding." The strange sensation that ran down our spines told us that our marriage plans were not ours alone.

We keep this aim at the center of our spiritual life: to do what we perceive to be the will of God. We chose the kinds of work we did because we felt called to them as a woman or man might be called to religious life in a convent or monastery. Deep inside, we felt that each of us was made to serve others in a specific way: Mary as a nurse and Tom as a teacher. Tom had finished his studies and had already been teaching for several years when we had our first child, and Mary had only one semester to go to finish her nursing degree.

After our son arrived, Tom was able to get a sabbatical leave with full pay for the spring term, so he could be free to stay at home and take care of the baby while Mary finished her studies to become a registered nurse. When she graduated in June she was pregnant with our second child.

The years went by and the children kept coming. After almost twenty years of marriage, we had ten — five boys and five girls. Tom's siblings set a precedent. Before we got married, his older sister already had eight — four boys and four girls — and his younger brother had six — three boys and three girls. We all felt happy, blessed to have large families.

Even though we never got the thirteen children we hoped for, the number thirteen was always special in our family. Mary was born on the thirteenth day of the month, as were four of our children. Some thought this was unlucky, but we didn't. Not that we didn't feel unlucky sometimes, for we had our moments of feeling inadequate as parents. At times the continuous demands on our time and energy felt overwhelming.

Almost every term Tom had to teach an extra course at night and two more during summer session as well. Most months we had to struggle to pay all our bills. When things got really tight, Mary would work part time at the local hospital.

People frequently asked, "How can you take care of so many kids?" We would respond, "God gives each person the grace that he or she needs: when we had one child, we got the grace to be parents of one, and when we had ten, we got the grace to handle ten. Thank God, the kids came one at a time!" We often wondered how parents could manage with twins or triplets. What helped us the most was this: we were regularly lifted up and encouraged by the concrete help we received from God's generosity, what we called Providence. We really believed what Jesus said applied to us: "Strive first for the kingdom of God and his righteousness, and all these things will be given to you as well" (Mt 6:33). This faith brought us much peace and much joy.

Family Planning

But not everyone was happy. Some even poked fun at us or criticized us for not using birth control. For instance, whenever we announced a pregnancy our elderly and rather grumpy next-door neighbor did not hesitate to lecture us on the population explosion and the need for family planning. At first we pointed out that since she had no children, we were merely balancing things out. When that didn't impress her, we tried a lighter approach — "We do observe family planning: we had a boy, then a girl; a boy, then a girl; a boy, then a girl — all carefully planned, you see." She didn't even crack a smile. Finally, we had to tell her the whole truth: we really believe that each of these children is destined to live forever, and even though the world might be a bit more crowded down here for a time, there would be no crowding in the vast and endless spaces of eternity. She didn't say too much after that. She really did not believe that anything existed beyond the natural world. We had another perspective on things. In spite of these differences, however, the relationship with this neighbor slowly blossomed.

When this same neighbor's husband died, she decided to return to Europe where he was born, to spread his ashes and to remain there herself. When she put her house up for sale, she asked if we wanted to buy some of her furniture. At that time, in the late 1960s, we had no dining-room set, only a small ugly table with a home-made extension board that didn't match. Someone had given us that table along with a few odd chairs. When our neighbor invited us into her home, we saw that her dining room was the same size as ours but was filled with extraordinary furniture — an exquisite table with two extension boards neatly hidden inside, six padded chairs, a fine china cabinet, all in matching dark maple and in perfect condition. We felt uneasy because it was much too fine for us; we probably could not afford the table alone, which was our greatest need.

Our neighbor saw right away how much we admired everything and asked, "What do you think the table and chairs are worth?" We didn't know what to say. Even though the set was very old, its condition made it so valuable that an antique dealer might easily charge more than $500. But we felt we should offer no more than what we could afford, so at the risk of insulting her — and making ourselves look foolish — Tom whispered, "We can only afford $50." Our neighbor showed no reaction and stood there thinking for a moment. We were thinking too, "We must have insulted her!" What she said next astounded us: "When I bought this whole set second-hand after we got married, I paid $50 for it. Now it's so much older, so I really can't charge you that much. It wouldn't be fair." Tom quickly said, "We think it's worth much more and we'd love to have it." She thought some more and then replied, "Okay, but only if you agree to take the whole set plus these four side chairs and the two matching bookcases too. Otherwise I don't think it's fair." We agreed, of course! We also thought it wasn't fair; we knew it was a gift from heaven.

We got Providence!

Other stories in this book recount how we managed to meet our needs — both the basic and the extraordi-

nary. With every child came gifts we could not account
for in human terms alone. Even though these gifts
arrived week after week and year after year, we never
got used to them. They always came as a surprise. And
when they came, the children would often cry out:
"Hey, guys, we got Providence!"

What is Providence? Does it have a real impact on
our daily lives? Or is it merely a dream, a pious idea?
We have been asking ourselves these questions for
many years. When we look back on our experiences
we find a single thread that runs through them all —
a golden thread that not only links the experiences
together, but that suggests a higher relationship too.
We are still trying to understand the real meaning of
Providence. Over and over, we found that it always
seemed to be mysterious, and always full of surprises.
Providence seemed to be connected to what was
most precious and most strange in our lives, not so
much what we were doing as what God was doing.

Somehow, in special ways God works in our world
to change our lives. Especially when we try to do God's
will and add a divine dimension to our human actions,
we get the hundredfold that God promised. We think
of Providence first as the actions of God as a provider,
as a father who looks ahead to take care of the needs
of his children. We also think of Providence as the
provisions themselves that arrive from God, often in
unexpected, unique ways that surprise us with their
divine simplicity and originality. In contrast to the cold,
impersonal actions of absolute and deterministic Fate
or Destiny, Providence seems warm and personal,
always considerate of our choices as agents who are
human and thus really free. Two passages from Chiara
Lubich's *Essential Writings* convey what we mean.

> Pope Paul VI teaches us that this true life of
> Christians transfers them to a higher sphere,
> in which greatness, nobility, an atmosphere
> of paradise reigns, radically transforming an
> otherwise flat and colorless existence: "The
> grand designs of God, the undertakings that
> the Lord's providence proposes for human
> destinies can coexist with and inhabit the most
> ordinary conditions of daily life." (69)

We realize that our family is quite "ordinary" and
sometimes quite "flat and colorless," but we also realize
that the extraordinary blessings we have received have
lifted us to "a higher sphere." When we fully correspond
to these blessings, we feel God is near, and we live for a
time in "an atmosphere of paradise."

> If everyone did nothing but God's will at
> every moment without hesitation, not going to
> extremes, they would see fulfilled before their
> very eyes God's plan for people and things, for
> families and nations, for religious groups and
> for the world: they would share in, as specta-
> tors and actors, the unfolding of the mysteries
> of Providence on earth. (76)

God has dealt gently with our family. He made it
easier for us to believe because again and again he let
us feel his palpable presence and glimpse "the mysteries
of Providence" right at home.

This little book records some of God's gifts to our
family. We wrote it to say thanks.

Reflections

God seems to prefer not to perform miracles in accomplishing his goals but to work through nature, through us, in order to manifest his Providence. William Shakespeare, like other great writers, was aware that people often do not take advantage of opportunities to cooperate with God and make his Providence known.

The hero in *King Lear* had to lose every opportunity he had as monarch before he could see clearly how human actions can participate in the acts of God and how one person's neglect of this, blindness to the noble calling to work with God, can prevent others from seeing and sharing in God's goodness. If we were as generous as we should be, King Lear discovered, we would "show the heavens more just." If we would take care of the poor, the poor in spirit as well as the poor in material goods, the poor — and all of us — might see God's Providence in a new way. Lear realized that he had failed to do this, that as a proud king he did not feel what the poor felt and did not let them share in his excess wealth:

> *O, I have ta'en*
> *Too little care of this! Take physic, pomp;*
> *Expose thyself to feel what wretches feel,*
> *That thou mayst shake the superflux to them*
> *And show the heavens more just.*

> (III, IV, 32-36)

Like anyone who is too full of self, King Lear needed to take a "physic" to purge his own vanity or "pomp" and learn to pay more attention to others, to people in need, so that he could "shake" or distribute his surplus (or "superflux") to them. Unfortunately, only after his evil daughters took away all his wealth and power and locked him out on a stormy night did Lear gain the insight that changed his life. Through his suffering, he realized the human responsibility to work with God by caring for his children, thereby revealing the justice of his Providence.

People can act as true agents of God's Providence. Whether they realize it or not, people do have the power to help reveal God's generosity by being generous with the gifts that God has distributed to them. Whenever they do that, they "show the heavens more just."

Questions

1. What do you think of when you hear the word "Providence"?
2. Is faith in a loving God necessary before we can see the actions of Divine Providence in the world?
3. Did you ever lose something you considered valuable and then later discover other things that are more important?
4. How can you "show the heavens more just" in your own life?

1

Two Apartments
and a Big Old House

There is a special providence in the fall of a sparrow.

HAMLET

We began our married life with very little. We had lots of debts — student loans as well as personal debts to pay each month. We had to live on a very tight budget, so we lived together in the small, partially furnished attic apartment above a private home that Tom had rented not far from where he worked in Brooklyn.

Where does he sleep?

When our first child arrived during our first year together, we had to put him in a dresser drawer because we could not afford a crib. He was a happy baby who seldom cried; he was almost always smiling or sleeping. He never seemed to mind not having a crib and the drawer was the cozy place he seemed to like best.

Our landlord and his wife were very quiet, retired people who rented the attic rooms to Tom only because he was a teacher who promised to be quiet too and, as the landlady stipulated, "not have any wild parties with wild music." We never heard any sounds from their part of the house. When we handed them the rent money each month, we spoke no more than a few words. We were afraid they would resent a baby coming into the peaceful sanctuary of their home.

A few days after we brought the baby home, however, our landlady shocked us by climbing up to the third
floor and knocking at our door. She asked bluntly, "Do
you have a crib for the baby?" When we said we didn't,
she asked, "Well, where does he sleep?" Tom answered,
"In the second drawer, for now." She thought a minute.
Tom was holding the baby, who seemed to warm her
heart. She then started telling us about her daughter
who once lived in this attic apartment and raised her
two children here. She added that when her daughter
moved out she left some things in the basement that
she no longer wanted. "Would you like a crib and a
high chair?" she asked. We were so speechless we could
only nod our heads. As she started down the stairs, she
turned and said, "Could you use a playpen too?" Thus
with our first child our gifts from Providence continued.

Do you want to save a trip?

The following year, we decided we had to move to
New Jersey. Tom had been teaching long enough to
take a one-semester sabbatical leave with full pay. Mary
needed one semester of full-time study to complete
the requirements for becoming a registered nurse. So
we found an apartment near St. Joseph's Hospital in
Paterson, where she had been studying before we got
married. Our plan was that during the day, while she
was in school, Tom would take care of the baby and try
to study during his naps.

The move was rather easy since apart from the baby
furniture we inherited, we had only a few possessions.
The new landlady told us that the previous tenants
would move out in the morning and we could move
in the same afternoon. When we arrived they were still

carrying some of their furniture out and apologized for making us stand out on the sidewalk. They were a young couple and seemed very friendly. At one moment the husband, who was carrying out a fine old-fashioned man's dresser, stopped to rest a moment. "We got this from the Salvation Army second-hand store when we moved in here. We don't need it anymore so we're bringing it back. There's also a matching women's dresser upstairs with a large mirror to go with it." He was rubbing his hand across its smooth maple finish as he said, "It still looks like new, doesn't it? It sure served us well."

Tom heard a little voice inside urging, "Ask him. Say something!" Too embarrassed to ask him outright, he could only mutter, "Do you want to save a trip?" The man smiled and replied, "Could you use this dresser? You can have the other one too." Mary, who was holding the baby in her arms, kept nodding her head up and down. Tom told him, "The only dresser we own is a little one for the baby." The man said, "That settles it then. Can you help me bring this back upstairs? Thanks to you, our moving out is already done!" Tom replied, "And, thanks to you, we're already partly moved in!"

A handyman's special

We stayed in New Jersey for a few months after Mary graduated from nursing school. During those months, Tom's father came for a visit. Tom tells the story:

* * *

DAD WANTED TO RIDE ALONG WITH ME TO BROOKLYN, WHERE I was still working. We had to drive through the Lincoln Tunnel and pass through Manhattan to get to the

Brooklyn Bridge. My dad was a police reporter who chased after stories all over Chicago, but even that did not prepare him for the fast pace of Manhattan traffic. Although he tried to hide it, he was really frightened, especially by the cabs coming from all directions. "You can't keep doing this every day. I'll be worried sick about you when I go back home. Why don't you move closer to your job?"

I tried to explain: "I don't mind it. I'm used to this kind of driving. I even enjoy the competition!" But Dad was not amused, so I quickly added, "Seriously, the real reason is that we can't afford such a large apartment in New York. Soon we'll have two kids. We'll really need the space we have here in New Jersey."

When we got back home that evening, Dad raised the subject again and again: "What you really have to do is move close to where you work. What you need if you're planning to have more kids, is a house — a house near where you work." "Yes," I quickly replied, "that would be wonderful. But it's impossible now. We have no savings and still have student loans to pay off. Who would give us a mortgage? It's simply not possible!" Dad would not give up: "Listen to me. It won't hurt to look at the homes for sale around your school and see what they cost. It can't hurt to look. Do me a favor, do it as soon as you can and then call me and let me know. I'll help you as much as I can. Remember, I won't sleep at night until you do something."

So Dad went back to Chicago, and we went house hunting in Brooklyn. We did it to love him, for we had no hope of finding something we could afford. For several weekends Mary and I kept the area's realtors busy showing us the big Victorian homes near my school, in neighborhoods like Flatbush and Midwood. They all seemed too big and much too expensive. We finally found one a bit smaller than the others that needed a lot of work. It was a "handyman's special," as they say in the advertisements, and I was pretty handy. Before becoming a teacher I had worked as a house painter, a laborer doing cement work, and an apprentice plumber.

At first glance, the house seemed huge, more like a mansion. It had five bedrooms, three average-sized ones and two very large ones, and three bathrooms. It also had a nice little yard and a two-car garage. To us apartment dwellers it seemed incredibly opulent. We thought we would never be able to fill it, since at the time we had only a little furniture, one child, and a second one on the way. We could only dream of owning a place like this. Since all we really had were debts, it was something to pray for.

On the outside, the house's siding and chipped stucco were crudely painted an ugly "battleship grey and toolhouse green," as a neighbor described it. Its well-worn roof needed to be replaced right away. The interior was even uglier: the dark rose walls in every room needed plastering as well as painting, the blackened hardwood floors needed sanding, the top-floor shower leaked into the bedroom below, and the full basement still had an old pot-bellied coal furnace that someone had "modernized" with an oil jet burner. Half of the large basement was taken up with a smelly oil tank on one side and a coal bin with lots of coal dust on the other. A neighbor told us that when it rained hard, the basement flooded.

Its poor condition did not frighten us away. It attracted us because we dreamed that it might bring the price down low enough that even we might afford it.

This ugly place also attracted us because it was only two blocks from my school and the neighbors on each side were older teachers with whom I worked. One of them, whom I knew well, filled us in about the house, the other neighbors, and the many advantages there would be if we lived there.

We then had a long talk with the realtor. He admitted he had a personal interest in getting the property for us since his daughter lived on the block and he sometimes worked for my school. He told us frankly that the housing market was very slow at that time, and that he and the owner hoped to make a quick sale. The price was set at $40,000, which was comparable to the other houses we had looked at. To someone like me making less than $10,000 per year, it seemed astronomic.

I told the realtor, "I think that price is much too high for us. The house needs so much work, and will soon need a new roof and a new furnace." The realtor did not seem to pay attention to what I said. He explained, "The owner lives in Philadelphia, and he's very anxious to sell it quickly because he's getting tired of having to go back and forth to take care of the place. Why don't you make him an offer?" I replied, "What should I say? How low do you think we could go?" "Why don't you offer him $30,000, and see what he says." We both assumed that cutting the price by a quarter would lead him to start coming down a little in the price, perhaps to $39,000 or $38,000.

A few days later, the realtor called. "I just got off the phone with the owner. I told him what you said about the old furnace, the smelly oil tank and filthy coal bin and how you wanted to make that area into a playroom for the kids. He has kids and understands. I also told him about the roof and all the plastering and painting that had to be done. When he asked where you worked, I told him you were a teacher and didn't earn very much. When I thought he was prepared for the worst, I told him you could offer only $30,000. After a long silence, he said 'If that's the best you can do, you can tell them that will be okay.' "

The realtor was as amazed as we were. We phoned Dad right away, and he was too. He could hardly believe we could buy such a big house for such a low price. He was glad we got the ball rolling and told us to go right to the nearest bank and find out how much we'd need for a down payment to get a mortgage. We found the best we could do was get a twenty-year mortgage with a $10,000 down payment. Where could we get so much money — more than I made all year?

We were feeling rather hopeless and sad. What made it worse was that we would have to tell Dad that it wouldn't work out, and that he would be very disappointed. And he seemed so when we told him the bad news. All he could say was, "Let me think about it. I'll see what I can do. I'll call you back tomorrow." We didn't feel he would be able to do anything. The next day he called, "Here's what your mother and I decided: we'll come up with the down payment and you can pay us back a little each month. Then we'll stop worrying about you guys and be able to sleep at night."

*   *   *   *   *   *

We've been in that house for over forty years; seven children have moved into their own places now, three are still here with us, and the house, well over a century old, looks better than ever.

We are all convinced that God had a plan for us and our children, a plan that included this big old house. Looking back at the steps we were led to take in order to get it, we see his Providence in action. We are most grateful because this is one of his biggest gifts to our family.

Reflections

Divine Providence fascinated many great writers of the English Renaissance. In addition to Shakespeare, there were the epic poet John Milton and the lyric poet George Herbert. Milton wrote *Paradise Lost* in order to "assert eternal Providence and justify the ways of God to men," as he said at the beginning; he ended his epic with Adam and Eve leaving the Garden of Eden with "Providence their guide."

In the poem "Providence," George Herbert, a saintly young Anglican priest, viewed all things as governed by divine power. He thought all humans must praise Providence, because of all creation they alone have the knowledge and skill to speak: "Man is the world's high priest: he doth present / the sacrifice for all." He also thought that those who had the talent to write, a gift from Providence itself, have a special obligation to sing the praises of Providence, whom he addressed as a divine person:

> *O Sacred Providence, Who from end to end*
> *Strongly and sweetly movest! Shall I write,*
> *And not of Thee, through Whom my fingers*
> *   bend*
> *To hold my quill? Shall they not do Thee right?*

As he was moving his pen across the page, Herbert realized that he could do so only through the energy of God's Providence. As a consequence, he had to sing praise about what was moving him because that is God's "right."

Herbert also realized that because it is the "power and love" of God, Providence acts both "strongly and sweetly."

> *We all acknowledge both Thy power and love*
> *To be exact, transcendent, and divine;*
> *Who dost so strongly and so sweetly move,*
> *While all things have their will, yet none but Thine.*

George Herbert and other poets of his day were enchanted by how, with his hidden "power and love," God moves all things. At the same time he saw that we humans have the power to move freely as we choose. How these powers work in harmony is a deep mystery. This must be so: since the actions of Providence involve both what happens in heaven and what happens here on earth, what is supernatural and what is natural, such actions cannot be fully understood by us on earth.

In the more secularized contemporary world, it is more difficult to see what Shakespeare, Milton, and Herbert saw in Providence. If, however, we look deep inside of creation, both in nature and in ourselves, if we ask what moves it all, what brought it to be and holds it in being, what gave it life and keeps it breathing each moment — if we look at our little finger, for instance, and consider that if God stopped loving it right this minute, it would simply disappear — we may recapture some of the wisdom that those wise poets had. We might even discover how Providence is working in our lives right now "so strongly and so sweetly." We may realize as we think about our own experiences how they

have been shaped by the "power and love" of our most
generous God.

Questions

1. Do you ever feel the need to praise God for those
   who cannot do so?
2. Have you ever felt or done something so new and
   surprising that you wondered where in the world
   it came from?
3. How has God's "power and love" affected your life?
4. How did you first learn about Divine Providence?

2

Clothes and Toys and Cars

*Therefore do not worry, saying, "What will we eat?
...What will we wear?" ... Your heavenly Father
knows that you need all these things.*

MT 6:31-32

We had to figure out over and over how to find clothes for so many people. Right away, we invested in a sewing machine, so that Mary could make clothes for the children, especially when they were small. She also made curtains and drapes, and even replaced the fabric on our worn-out couches. We soon found out, however, that we had a Gift-giver in Heaven who wanted to resolve even the little problems with us.

Providence came most frequently in the form of clothing and toys. We seldom purchased new clothes for ourselves and for the children, not only because we could not afford to but more because we didn't have to. Here are only a few of our many stories about this.

Good friends ... instruments of God

Tom and his close friend, Simon, went to college together. Simon got a well-paying government job, and because they were unable to have children, his wife also worked. Tom and Simon wear exactly the same size clothes. Tom never cared much about having new clothes or wearing the latest fashions, but Simon loved to be in style so he changed most of his wardrobe every year. He and his wife loved to go shopping and often bought more than they really needed. Tom explains:

*   *   *

WHENEVER I WENT TO VISIT SIMON, HE WOULD ASK ME TO TRY ON one of his shirts or a suit that he no longer wore. Inevitably he would say, "Tom, it looks great on you! In fact, it fits you better than it does me! Do you want it?" It seems like every time we saw each other he would give me some more clothes. He was so fussy that he kept his clothes in perfect condition, and since he had so many and shared them with me, we both had clothes that always looked brand new.

I knew Simon so well that I understood that he really wanted to be a good caretaker of God's gifts and did not want to waste any of them. At the same time, he had a strong passion for collecting things. I often noticed that this passion got out of hand and he would buy things that he didn't use. Then when I would come for a visit and he offered to share these extra things with me, I noticed a visible sign of relief when he saw that I could use them — in fact, that I really needed them. His uneasiness at having too much was assuaged by his generosity to me. I sometimes wondered whether he felt more free to buy two or three shirts at a time instead of just one so that he could try them all out and then pass on to me the ones he would not be able to wear. In fact, I would sometimes fantasize that if I weren't there in need, he would have to curtail his love of shopping or he would have to rent storage space to house all his purchases! In some strange way, we helped each other grow in virtue — me in humility and him in generosity.

And then Simon and his wife had to move to California because of his job. But even then, the Providence kept coming. At least once a year, I would get a big box packed with shirts and slacks and jackets and ties — often in the latest or near-latest styles. Very often, as I was getting dressed in the morning, I would remember that the shirt or tie I was putting on came from my friend, and this would remind me to say something like this, "May God bless Simon for sharing with me."

When Simon died of cancer a few years ago, his wife gave me many of his clothes, like my bathrobe and many ties, so I continue to pray for him and her each time I put them on. I feel that his love for me continues beyond the grave in all the signs he left behind and in my love and prayers for him. I know that these people were not only good friends, but were instruments of God's love for me.

*   *   *   *   *   *

Bargain basements

Families with several children often sense that other people think they must be in need of something. That was proved to us many times. For example, neighbors we never met would come to our front door, introduce themselves, then say, "I have only one child, and he's growing too big for his tricycle. Would your children like to have it?" And of course the kids did like to have it. We were always short of bikes. Another would come and say, "My girl has outgrown these clothes. I hate to throw them out. They are still almost new. Would your girls fit into them?" Since we had five girls, at least one of them would be the right size.

As teenagers, some of our older girls became highly fashion conscious and wanted us to buy what all the other girls were wearing. We found, however, that the fashionable brands were much more expensive than ordinary jeans and way beyond our budget. Of course they were quite disappointed: "Everyone on our block and all the kids at school have Jordache Jeans! Why can't we?" We took advantage of such moments, to explain some aspects of our family budget, to help the children understand why we couldn't buy everything they wanted. Very often and always to our surprise, however, Providence would arrive with exactly what they were wishing for.

Two of our friends, Tom and Marie, lived a few blocks away. Tom had a good job in Manhattan and Marie stayed home to raise their two daughters. These girls, who were old enough to babysit our children, always dressed in the latest fashions.

One afternoon Marie arrived with her daughters and said with some embarrassment: "My girls keep buying new clothes and never seem to wear out the ones they already have. We don't know what to do with the clothes they don't wear anymore. I hope you won't feel insulted if we offer them to your girls." Mary's eyes lit up. "We'd love to have them! And what our girls can't fit into, we can pass on to others." Relieved and happy, Marie handed Mary several shopping bags full of clothes.

As soon as Marie left, Mary called out, "Look what just came from Marie!" Our daughter Jennie was the quickest. She came running down the stairs, calling out, "Hey, guys, we've got Providence!" When Mary and the girls started sorting out the piles of clothes, their excitement reminded Tom of a comedy about women pushing each other aside at the bargain counter in Macy's basement. It was a wild scene. Suddenly he heard Jennie scream above the other voices: "Look what I found. Jordache Jeans, two pairs of Jordache Jeans! One's my size! The other one will fit Chrissy!"

After Mary told Marie how happy the children were with her daughters' gifts, Marie started a tradition: every year she came with bags of clothes that her daughters outgrew or, more often, got tired of wearing. The packages arrived so regularly that it seemed as if the children were getting things they ordered themselves through the mail.

The greatest finds

One day when the children were playing in front of the house, a man we didn't know came up on the porch where Tom was reading and said, "Excuse me. I'm your neighbor. My house is across the street, a few houses down the block, the green one, over there. I see you have lots of small children. I wonder if they would like some of the things I have collected over the years. They now lay scattered around in my backyard." Tom was quite surprised and said, "Wow, that's very nice of you!" The man said, "Would you like to see them now?"

So Tom and a couple of the oldest children followed the man into his backyard. They didn't see much at first because the grass had grown so tall. Then, sticking up above the grass, they were surprised to see horses' heads and other strange shapes of iron and wood. The man urged, "Go ahead and look around! You can have whatever you want." The children waded in and uncovered a big handsome horse that lacked its half-moon rockers. It reminded us of the prancing horses on carousels. Then they found a smaller one that hung on its steel frame with springs. Of course the children wanted them both. "You can fix the bottom of the big one, can't you, Daddy?" Tom replied right away, "I think I have just the wood to make some rockers." Their delight brought a huge smile on the man's face.

One of the greatest finds in this treasure hunt came when the children uncovered an old-fashioned, heavy steel tractor, the kind that hasn't been made for many years. It was a bit rusty but it was a perfect replica of a John Deere, with a wide steel seat and high yellow engine that supported the steering wheel. The man said, "Take that too, but I think the chain needs fixing." He even helped them carry all these antique toys into our garage so Tom could begin working on them. For many years afterwards, whenever little children came into our yard, they would jump up on the horses. Many boys would head straight to the tractor and wait in line to take turns driving it. Although the two horses were eventually stolen — we hope that they continue to delight other children — our grandchildren still wait in line to drive the old steel tractor. Unfortunately, that generous neighbor moved away soon after, but we all knew he was important, a special agent of Divine Providence for us.

Even though we had little in our budget for clothes and toys, an abundance of them always seemed to be coming from such agents of Providence. What we could not use we donated to clothing drives in local churches. Sometimes our whole family organized a porch sale and gave the proceeds to a project for the poor. We made sure that the goods circulated. We tried to be like the plants that take from the ground only what they need to live.

Each evening, when we prayed together, one of the children would name the generous persons who brought us gifts that day and who showed us once again how much God loves us.

No money and no trade in

Over the years we've had many cars and vans, their sizes determined by the number of people in the family. For the first few years we owned a little Renault 10, but we had to make the back seat into a playpen and put most of our luggage on the roof rack, making the tiny car look top-heavy and unsafe. When our fourth child was born, we realized we needed a much bigger car.

We bought a Dodge station wagon from a man who advertised it as "Like new, with very low mileage." He told us, "This car belonged to my sister. She didn't use it much and took good care of it." Even though it was over five years old, it had only 30,000 miles on the odometer. It was a clean car and he seemed to be honest. In his apartment, we discussed it further in front of his wife and small children. He appeared to be a fine family man as well. After we closed the deal and walked back to the car, however, one thing raised a doubt. Twice, he said, "I think you should change the hoses. The car is, after all, over five years old." We never heard of changing hoses after only 30,000 miles.

The car ran well for about a year, but then it began to need so many repairs that we suspected it had a lot more than 40,000 miles. One day the police came to the house as part of a fraud investigation regarding the man who sold us the station wagon. He had been arrested as part of a ring that worked with a car dealer, taking old cars that had been traded in, turning back the odometers, then selling them at inflated prices. A few months later the newspaper carried that man's picture, with a story about his arrest and conviction. Someone suggested that we sue him to get our money back. Mary was not so sure that this was a good plan. Shortly before, one of our neighbors had been shot and killed as he got in his car to go to court to testify against some mobster. "What if the guy who sold us the car was also in the mob?" she said. "I don't think we should do anything. What we need is a new car!" But we had no money and no trade in either. In good conscience, we could not sell the station wagon to anyone else.

Our elderly next door neighbors had taught at the same school with Tom, and had become close friends of our family. Since both husband and wife were retired, they spent a lot of time with us, especially on holidays. Their only child was a priest, so they became like grandparents to our children. One of our little girls, who often played for hours with the lady, exclaimed one time, "She is my closest friend!"

This day, the husband was telling Tom how they were worried about our driving such a car because it was breaking down so often. They were particularly worried about the trip we were planning to Miami to visit Mary's father. "We don't think it's safe to drive that car from New York all the way to the bottom of Florida. You really need to buy a new car." When Tom reminded them that we could not afford it, he said, "Why don't you look around and find the car that will suit your growing family, just to see how much it would cost?" Even though in his heart he felt that it wouldn't amount to anything, out of love for his neighbor, Tom agreed to look.

We found a car that was perfect for the family, a nine-passenger Chevy Impala station wagon. It was expensive, though — $6,000 — at the time almost half of our yearly income! So we went back to our neighbors, certain that announcing this ridiculously high price would surely stop them from encouraging us to get a new car. But that's not what happened.

We found the neighbors on the front porch where they usually sat in the afternoon and told them what a new car would cost. They looked at us for a moment in silence and then the husband got up and went into the house without saying a word. We talked with his wife about other things and a few minutes later the husband came out and handed us a check for $6,000. All he said was "Go buy the car so we won't have to worry about the children. You can pay us back whenever you can." We were absolutely flabbergasted.

When summer came, we had a great vacation with grandpa in Florida. Somehow — little by little — we managed to put together enough money to pay back the loan even before the year was out.

These same neighbors helped us even after they passed away. They had an old car — a Dodge Dart — that still ran well. Their son said," I think my parents would want your kids to have the car." Of course the older kids were ecstatic because they recently had gotten their driver's licenses and didn't like borrowing the big station wagon that we needed for the rest of the family. They loved the Dart and called it "The Derby" because it was shaped something like the hat. They liked to race it all around Brooklyn.

Our next vehicle came in time for our California vacation.

Reflections

Accumulating possessions seems so ingrained in the American way of life that it appears to be a habit that's impossible to avoid. We seem to end up having too many things. Even when we recognize that we really don't need a particular item, we hold onto it and instinctively come up with reasons why we should: "I might need it some day." "Just in case I lose the one I have." And then we hide it in a safe place so we don't have to worry about someone stealing it. And then we forget we have it.

At the same time we all know that giving things away is good. We know that giving a gift makes us happy, even happier than it makes the person we give it to. There is something sublime about giving gifts. There is something divine in it. This is probably because we know that the greatest giver of gifts is God himself. Deep down we know that throughout our lives everything we possess has been a gift.

Still, we worry about many things. We worry about not having some things and we worry about not using well the many things we have. And we feel that it's right to worry about our children and our community and our country. Perhaps we can get some relief from our worries if we look more closely at what the gospel says about worrying.

The logic of the gospel often seems to turn things on their head. Many times Jesus said, "Don't worry!" and then he explained why:

> Therefore, I tell you, do not worry about your life, what you will eat or what you will drink, or about your body, what you will wear. Is not life more than food, and the body more than clothing? Look at the birds of the air; they neither sow nor reap nor gather into barns, and yet your heavenly Father feeds them. Are you not of more value than they? And can any of you by worrying add a single hour to your span of life? (Mt 6:25-27)

How do these words impact us who worry so much about so many things? Jesus is teaching us that in itself, worrying is quite useless. It does no good and may do the opposite by bringing on nothing but aggravation and stress and sleepless nights. In short, we must try to avoid it. But how can that be done?

Jesus suggests that we think more about how our "heavenly Father" takes care of the birds and the other parts of his creation. Jesus wants us to understand that God is a real parent like our earthly fathers and mothers and that we rational creatures, who are his children, have to ask him for what we need:

> Is there anyone among you who, if your child asks for bread, will give a stone? Or if the child asks for a fish, will give a snake? If you then, who are evil, know how to give good gifts to your children, how much more will your Father

in heaven give good things to those who ask him! (Mt 7:9-11)

How then can we control our worrying? It seems that the best way — perhaps the only way — is to have the simplicity of little children who have complete trust in their heavenly Father and who ask their heavenly Father to take care of all the things they worry about.

Questions

1. How do you deal with strong urges to shop for the latest fashions or shop for the newest technology?
2. Are we not all poor in some ways and rich in others? Can we enrich each other?
3. How can children experience generosity from their relatives and neighbors in order to learn about the generosity of God?
4. Do you worry about many things and fail to trust in the heavenly Father?

3

Vacations:
California & Others

If God sends you, he'll pay your expenses.

HAITIAN PROVERB

God really wants us to be happy. His Providence extends beyond our basic needs, even to our recreations and vacations. Sometimes we have to be patient and wait.

For about five years we planned a cross–country vacation, but each year we had to shelve our plans for lack of funds. During those years we had to be satisfied with much shorter vacations. We never lost our desire to go out West, however, and each year we could think of more reasons for going. There were two main ones.

First, we felt a need to visit the widely scattered members of our family. Just to mention a few of them, our children had never met most of their cousins and some of their aunts and uncles. Tom had not seen his youngest brother, who lives in Colorado, since their father's funeral ten years before. Mary's sister moved to Los Angeles and had not visited us for seven years. We had relatives and close friends all across the country, from New York to California.

Second, we were convinced that learning about one's country through firsthand experience has enormous educational value. We wanted our children to have that experience. We wanted it for ourselves too, for although we read about United States history and geography, we had not yet had the chance to see very much of the rich variety and beauty of our vast country.

Every winter for those five years we would begin planning our California trip, and then every summer we found that we could not afford to go, no matter how carefully we saved our tax refunds and the extra income Tom got for teaching summer school. Moreover, since the family grew larger every couple of years, the trip seemed less and less likely. By the time our tenth child arrived, we had outgrown our nine-passenger station wagon. We could no longer squeeze their little bodies into the two back seats, and new state laws required bulky car seats for the babies. We looked into renting a minibus or a camper but found out that the cost exceeded our means.

Surprising events ... real happenings

Then in the spring of 1986 a series of surprising events changed our dreams into real happenings. The first one came with a phone call from a close friend of the family informing us that he and his wife had given up house-hunting for the time being and that they would like us to use the $14,000 they had been saving for a down payment to buy the van that we had been wishing for. Deeply moved, we gratefully accepted this special providence from God, a sure sign of his love.

After looking around for the best deal, we found a twelve-passenger van for $14,000 that seemed perfect for our family. Each person had a seat, and a seatbelt. We finally were legal, too, since our state law required that all children under four had to be in car seats or booster seats.

The following year, our friends found a house they wanted to purchase and needed the money they had loaned to us. At the same moment, the personnel office at Tom's school informed all the teachers that for a number of years excess funds had been deducted from their salaries and that at any time the money could be refunded. All of us were amazed at this news. When Tom went to draw out the money, he was told that $14,000 was available. Tom got goose bumps right away and so did the rest of us when he got home to tell us. We never could figure out why all that money had accumulated, but we could see that it was part of God's plan — we got it when our generous friends and we needed it most.

Cross-country planning

Having a big van in which we could ride comfortably provoked an enthusiastic return to our cross-country plans.

As a trial run, we took a trip to visit Mary's father, who had just moved to South Carolina. We found that we had enough room to travel comfortably even when we were on the road for thirteen hours each way. And since our oldest son, who had just turned eighteen, was now an experienced highway driver, we felt secure with three of us able to take turns behind the wheel. Thus, all through the winter of 1986–87 we planned our California trip, but we hesitated to tell our relatives that we were coming because one big hurdle still remained: how would we find the money to pay for the gas and tolls and the food, not to mention the motels? We had already given up the idea of camping, since we lacked equipment, reservations, and especially know-how.

It wasn't until May that this problem was solved, and again it was by a surprising act of Providence.

Tom had been working as the summer deputy for his department at school. Not long before the start of the summer session, one of the teachers scheduled to teach Renaissance Drama told him, "I have this great offer to teach in Europe this summer. What should I do?" Tom quickly assured him, "Don't worry. Take that job. I'll find someone to replace you." But as the weeks went by, he could not find someone qualified. The department was reluctant to drop the course, since it was fully enrolled and some students needed it for their majors.

Then one afternoon, as he was thinking about how to finance the California trip and how to staff the summer course, a little voice within suggested a way to do both at once: ask for special permission to add this course to his already full teaching schedule. This would mean working hard to set up a new course during the extremely compact summer session, which allowed little time for study, but it would also mean earning enough extra money to pay for the trip. After talking it over with Mary and the older children, because it would mean working long hours during the months before the trip, he got their okay. The provost agreed to add the course to his schedule.

Once we felt we would have enough money, we started calling our relatives and friends across the country to arrange for our visits. Delighted, they began making suggestions about the best itinerary and about sights we should not miss on the way.

Since food and lodging between visits with family and friends would make up, by far, our largest expense, we thought at first that we would be able to afford the trip only by staying with them every chance we had, both on the way out and the way back. The more we talked about this, however, the more we realized that stopping so often to visit would drag out the trip, especially since the children would want to prolong their visits with the many cousins they had not seen in many years or had never seen at all. One night Mary said, "We may never get to California at all!" The same evening we made the decision to head straight for Los Angeles, visit people and places there for a week or so, and then stop off for visits with the others on a leisurely and more winding way back home. As it turned out, this proved to be wise.

We soon started making lists of the people and places we all wanted to see. First, a catalogue of relatives: sisters and brothers and their families in Los Angeles; Denver; Windsor, Colorado; and northern Illinois. Then we made a list of friends in Arizona, California, and Chicago that we hoped to see. We were invited to stay for a week or so with Tom's old friend Simon near Los Angeles. Finally, we listed all the places the children wanted to see. Disneyland and Universal Studios were their first choices, but these were quickly dropped after we figured out the entrance fees for our large family. Our other favorite places in California were the missions along the coast, especially the one in Santa Barbara, and Yosemite and Sequoia National Parks. In Arizona and New Mexico, the kids expressed little interest in famous tourist sites. In fact, when we visited the Grand Canyon on the trip west the children took a quick look and said, "It's just a big hole in the ground. We want to see the Indians!"

Seeing the sights

After four days on the road, we finally arrived at the home of Simon and his wife in Reseda, a suburb of Los Angeles. They treated us as their own immediate family. Our oldest son, Tommy, is their godson. Of course they wanted us to have as rich an experience as possible on our family vacation.

They were taken aback when we told them that we were not planning on going to Universal Studios and Disneyland because we could not afford such things. "How could you come all the way from New York and not see some of our main attractions?" they asked. Then they tried to persuade us in another way: "Surely you have to admit that the children would enjoy seeing how films and TV shows are made. That would be very educational." Finally, they gave us no choice: "We really want you all to go and we will be happy to pay for it!"

The next morning they sent us off with directions for the freeways and two hundred dollars. The children really got a kick out of seeing how Hollywood creates illusions on film, and they were particularly thrilled by the stuntmen's gunfights, the trained animals' tricks, and the shark used in the film Jaws. When we got back to our friends' house, they were happy to hear how we all enjoyed the day at Universal Studios. This was the first of several of our experiences of Providence on this trip.

A few days later we were telling other friends we were visiting about our plans to visit the national parks in the middle of the state. They suggested we let them contact a Chinese priest, Fr. Francis Cheung, a good friend of theirs in Fresno, which is close to Yosemite and Sequoia. When they phoned him, he immediately invited us to stay with him since he had plenty of room

in his rectory and would enjoy the visit. A few days later
we moved in, spending most of the days in the parks
and the evenings and early mornings with Fr. Francis.
In addition to providing us with the enormous providence of lodging, he also cooked us breakfast — his
specialty was fried rice — and took us for dinner at his
friend's Chinese restaurant. This friend would not allow
us to pay for anything. Fr. Francis was quite extraordinary, overflowing with love and wisdom and humor.
After our first day together, we felt we were part of his
natural family. Through him we experienced the great
love of God.

On the day before we left, Fr. Cheung introduced
us to a Franciscan friar who ran a mission for migrant
workers near Fresno. He told us that his people were
generous, always giving him supplies, more than he
could use. He said his car at that moment was packed
to the top and he would like to share with us.

In a few minutes the friar pulled his old car next to
ours and started handing us bags and bags of plump,
recently picked tree-ripened peaches. After a few bag-
fuls we tried to stop him, but he said, "What you can't
eat yourselves, you can give as gifts to those you visit as
you travel." Then, after filling almost every corner of
our van with peaches, he started on the almonds, bags
and bags of almonds. "These make nice gifts too!" he
said. He was tall and gaunt, very much how we imagined
St. Francis must have looked. He was always smiling, a
true man of poverty, so glad to be giving away all that
he had.

The Franciscan friar's gifts proved to be a special
boon for us. After we left him and Fr. Cheung, for several days we had peaches and almonds for snacks as well

as presents to give to everyone we met. They really were the most delicious ones we had ever tasted.

Happiest place on earth

When we returned to Los Angeles, another surprise awaited us. While we were visiting with friends in their home, in an adjoining room another of their guests, who had come from France, could not help but overhear our conversation. When we left, she told the people we had visited, "How could such a large family not include Disneyland in their vacation plans?" She was shocked to think that our many children would miss such a fun-filled place. "I'm leaving what I can for them. It's only seventy dollars. Maybe they can get the rest from someone else and take the kids to Disneyland." We never saw or heard from this woman again.

Later that day, when we arrived at Mary's sister's home, her sister said that her only child had been pestering her to take him to Disneyland for some time, but she could not take off from work. "Would you take him? He'd love to spend the day with his cousins. I'll be happy to help pay for the tickets." She also said that the husband of her close friend worked at Disneyland and could get us a discount. As all these things were developing, we realized that another unexpected sign of God's love was appearing. Of course we all had lots of fun with Mickey and his friends.

"I never heard of such a thing."

Because of Providence, every summer we found ways to take vacations in order to get away from the big city. One year we thought we'd like to spend a week in

New Hampshire. We were attracted by pictures of Lake Sunapee, with its clear waters and beautiful lakefront homes, some of which were for rent.

When we phoned a real estate agent, we discovered that big lakeside places there were renting for around $1,000 a week, and small cottages far from the water were not much less. We could afford no more than $300 per week. The realtor also said that all the homes on the lake were already booked up for the whole summer. Places at other lakes in New England also proved to be too expensive.

Summer was in full swing. We still thought that if God wanted us to vacation at Lake Sunapee, he would find a way. When we put everything into his hands and prayed about it, we felt better. We even called the real estate agent again. She said that one family backed out and that left a very beautiful new home right on the lake open for the second week in August, but the price was still $1,000 for the week.

Tom was listening to his little voice inside, which gave him an inspiration. He asked the agent, "Could you ask the owner some questions for us?" The agent said, "Sure, why not?" Then Tom said something he never thought of nor heard of before: "Ask her that if she doesn't find a renter by August first and the place will be empty for a week, would she consider lowering the price for a family from New York City that has several kids who are dying to get out of this hot place and spend a week in the country?" The words poured out of his mouth. Where they came from, Tom never could figure out because he is not really at all clever in dealings like this. The realtor was caught off guard, "This is rather unheard of around here. Still, I'd like to help your family, so I'll call the owner and see what I can do. What could I say would be your highest offer?" Tom said, "Our budget will let us go no higher than $300." The agent quickly answered, "She'll never go for that!" Tom persisted, "If the place is empty that week, she'll get nothing, but if we come she'll at least have $300." The agent seemed reluctant. Tom added, "And we'd take good care of the place too." The agent said she'd tell the owner exactly what Tom said but told him, "Don't bank on it."

A few days later, the realtor called again: "I never heard of such a thing. The owner actually agreed to give you the place for $300! I never heard of such a thing before this." All we could say was "Whoopee!" (and thanks to the Holy Spirit for the inspiration). As it turned out, that vacation was one of our best, a fabulous mansion with large grounds right on the water where we swam and fished and paddled all over in kayaks. We felt rich — and grateful.

Reflections

Our work is not only necessary for our survival so that we can pay our bills; it also gives us dignity. When our work matches our talents, it cannot but fulfill us and make us happy. For this gift we can be grateful to Divine Providence, the source of all good gifts. We need, however, to keep our balance and take care not to be too attached to our work.

Workaholics cause suffering, often without realizing they are doing so. They may consider that by staying late at the office they are doing something good for themselves and for their families. Such work, however, not only may be exhausting themselves, but gradually may be damaging their whole family. "My Dad is always at work or thinking about his job. He pays no attention to me. We never do anything together."

In addition to being too attached to work, work can get too attached to us. In the contemporary world, it no longer remains within the walls of our workplaces, but can follow us wherever we go. The "smart" phones in our hands and purses allow anyone to reach us at any time. Technology keeps pulling our minds back to our work, even violating private time, like family dinners.

Relationships, especially within a family, take time. They cannot be purchased like merchandise. If not built up over time and nurtured, they die. That's why family vacations need high priority, lest they be neglected or skipped for more quick and easy satisfactions like work or hobbies. Of course we should love our work, but we also should be detached from it so that it does not overwhelm our relationships with God and with each other.

Relationships can be difficult and full of risks and surprises, just as people are. That's why building and maintaining strong family relationships requires effort and attentiveness. Rich relationships require a person to be inventive, alert to others' needs, and above all to be open to change.

We have found that vacations provided the best time to build relationships in the family. While relaxing together, we were not distracted by our regular routines of work and school. We had time to look at each other and enjoy each other and help each other. Most of all, we found that during vacations we learned to love each other more deeply.

Questions

1. Have you ever considered your work as a gift of Providence?
2. What challenges have you faced in trying to keep a balance between work and family?
3. How have your holidays and vacations affected your family relationships?
4. How does your family promote the sharing of goods and experiences?

4

Education: From Elementary
to Graduate Schools

*Every generous act of giving, with every perfect gift, is
from above, coming down from the Father of lights.*

JAS 1:17

Not long ago at the dinner table we were telling
our youngest son Mark about this little book
that we were trying to put together. We asked him if he
remembered some experiences of Providence that he'd
like to add. Right away he offered this:

*　*　*

WHAT ABOUT ALL THE HELP YOU GOT WHEN YOU WANTED TO SEND
me to a private high school? That was when Dad started
getting Social Security. It was pretty funny because he
didn't even know that he would get extra for each child
under eighteen. Remember that? The tuition was $6,000
for the year when I started. And the social security payment for me, since I was only fourteen, was the same,
exactly $6,000. And then, remember, the next year when
the tuition was raised to almost $7,000, the Social Security
payment went up to almost that same amount. That was
a surprise! You covered my tuition for all four years that
way. That sure looks like a lot of Providence to me.

*　*　*　　*　*　*

Mark, by the way, was the only one of our children we could afford to send to a private high school. The other nine went to the public high school in our neighborhood.

Over the years as we raised our children we were asked again and again questions like these:

"Aren't you worried about having so many children to provide for?"

"How are you going to put them all through college?"

"Do you have an educational savings plan for each child?"

"How will you all make it on your teacher's salary?"

"We have only two little children and we are worried already. Aren't you?"

These questions came from good friends who were concerned about us and our children.

With our large family, it was impossible to put aside any savings for education. At times we barely had enough money to pay our monthly bills. In fact, our family budget always counted on Providence. Sometimes, Providence came from our pension fund and sometimes, in moments of dire need, from a home equity loan often repaid with more Providence. However, we trusted that God would help us when the time came for the children to go to college. We were certain that if he gave us these children, he would help us educate them. And he did.

Once we decided we were going to have as many children as God would give us — and we kept hoping for thirteen — as each child came we had to make lots of adjustments. When our oldest children reached kindergarten age, we decided that we would have to send them and their siblings to public schools from elementary level right through college. To do otherwise would mean both of us working full-time, and Tom probably working two jobs. That would mean leaving the children without the constant care of parents through their formative years. We were sure that this could not be what God wanted for them, or for us.

Two disasters

We knew we had to do our part as well. We had to search out the best schools we could find. New York City has lots of schools to choose from. Sometimes the ones we enrolled them in proved inadequate academically, and we had to move them to better ones. The first two schools we chose, for example, turned out to be disasters.

We enrolled our first child in the local elementary school, which was located right at the corner of our block. After a few weeks, as Tom was walking by the school on his way to work, he turned toward the playground when he heard loud, amplified voices yelling over and over, "Recess is over! Get in line right now!" Two teachers were holding bullhorns. One held her horn right in the face of a little boy and blasted her voice, "Recess is over! Why aren't you in your line?!" Tom was so shocked by this that he went right into the schoolyard and confronted the teacher: "Why are you doing this? Don't you know you'll destroy this child's hearing?" The teacher, annoyed, answered: "It's the only way to control these kids!" Then she continued yelling through the bullhorn. Tom rushed into the school building and asked to speak with the principal. He gave

Tom the same answer, even after Tom described how the teacher put her horn in the child's face: "It's the only way we can control these kids." Tom realized that this violent way of dealing with students was clearly the school policy — and no one was going to change it.

We could not leave our son in such an environment, so we enrolled him in our parish school, despite having to pay tuition. At first this school was much better, so in the next two years we enrolled two more of our children. But then we noticed that the school was changing rapidly. Our children told us they were bored. Our daughter confessed that she brought a book of her own to school, held it below the desktop and read it when the teacher was going over things she already knew quite well. The teachers were not at fault. What was happening was that the student population was changing rapidly in our parish school. More and more students spoke Spanish, French or another language at home, and struggled to use English in the classroom. The pace of instruction became slower and slower to help those students overcome the language deficit, leaving less and less time for the students who did not need such help. So we had to change schools again.

Public yet special

Luckily the older children were good students. We had them tested and they were admitted to special programs in a public school in Brooklyn, not too far from our home. We were promised that in order to keep them together in the same school their younger siblings would be given waivers to be admitted.

The special programs, funded by the Astor Foundation, gave the children all the benefits of an exclusive private school, like small classes, excellent teachers, and an unusually gifted principal. Mr. Greenberg was both very friendly and very strict. He always seemed to be smiling and was genuinely interested in "his kids" and everything they did. The children loved him. They respected him too. He would walk up and down the halls and pop in and out of classrooms, sometimes just to listen, sometimes encouraging his teachers, of whom he was proud and fond. Sometimes he reminded us of a doting father, and at others of a strong captain in charge of every part of his tight ship. Everybody loved "Mr. Greenberg" somewhat like they loved the Lord — with genuine affection, tinged with a bit of fear. He was an extraordinary administrator who surrounded himself with a team of exceptional teachers.

The six grades our children went through at this public school were certainly more enriching than we ever imagined. We are grateful for these substantial gifts.

Our local public high school was similar in many ways. The principal had some of Greenberg's gifts: a great love of his students and teachers, high standards, especially in the special programs in science and humanities, and an excellent rapport with parents. He fostered a strong music program, with a pop band, a jazz band, and a full orchestra. Each of our children learned to play one or more instruments: double bass, clarinet, oboe, flute, guitar, and violin.

What college are you going to?

College years presented some challenges. In the junior and senior years of high school, students — and also some parents — have one big preoccupation and recurring question: "What college are you going to?"

Our children were no different. Their teachers, school counselors, and classmates encouraged them to go away to college. The children all understood, however, that even though a couple of them would have preferred to go elsewhere, the answer to that question would most likely be "Brooklyn College or any other public college." Even though Tom taught there, Brooklyn College — locals call it "the poor man's Harvard" — charged our children tuition, but less than $4,000 per year. The children could earn a little in the summer or even throughout the year to help pay for some expenses, and we covered the rest. Some of them also received scholarships and got through college tuition-free. Mary remembers well our son Paul's experience.

* * *

PAUL WAS IN HIS SENIOR YEAR OF HIGH SCHOOL WHEN HE received a letter from Brooklyn College stating that he was eligible to apply for a Presidential Scholarship because of his good grades and excellent SAT scores. He was really excited and agreed to complete the application form which had to be submitted by 5:30 PM Friday of the same week. A few days later, I asked him if he completed and submitted the application yet and he answered, "Not yet." But he assured me that he would do it. Then again on another day, I asked him. Again, his answer was "Not yet."

So I became concerned because the deadline was coming up in twenty-four hours and he had not even begun to do his part. Then he told me that it would really be a waste of time to apply for the scholarship, because he was certain that he would not get it anyway. "There are pre-med students applying for the same scholarship. I'm sure they'll get it before me," he said. I pointed out that if it were the will of God, he would get the scholarship in spite of all the pre-med students applying. There was only one way to find out. He needed to do his part. He seemed to have a little change of heart when he heard about the will of God and promised to complete the application. Tom and I were praying that he would.

The next day, when he came home from school around 4:00 PM, I asked if he had submitted his application. The deadline was 5:30 PM that day. He said, "No." After thinking things over, he was more convinced that applying would just be a waste of his time. At that point, I did what I had resisted all along, which was to make him do it. He knew he had no way out. So he sat at the computer, completed the application, wrote his essay, walked to the Brooklyn College scholarship office, and handed in his application, just barely meeting the deadline.

Two weeks later, he received a phone call confirming that he had been chosen to receive one of the twenty-five Presidential Scholarships granted that year. He couldn't believe it. I said, "You see, will of God, Paul, and pretty good pay for one hour's work. $16,000 for four years of college tuition."

* * * * * *

Inexpensive or free public education because of scholarships was tremendous Providence. Their college dorm was our home — which cost nothing additional. Being at home had its challenges but it also came with many benefits, apart from the cost. Among them was the chance to have the children mature with the support of parents, especially beneficial for our many artist children who took a little longer to mature. The Focolare centers nearby afforded them the chance to participate, as often as possible and if they chose to, in Focolare youth activities in New York. During their college years, five of them even spent a semester or two at an international youth center in Italy. We saw them mature in their ability to build relationships among family members, especially their parents, and also with others. They came to understand the value of spirituality in their own lives as young adults. From our perspective, such education is priceless.

What happens after college? If they chose to go on to graduate or professional schools we promised to help them as much as we could when that time came. Did we ever think how we could possibly do that? Yes, perhaps for a moment, but fully aware that this concern has to be left in God's hands.

Providence came in so many different ways, sometimes in the form of a check and sometimes in offers of professional work like the job that Mary had for almost twenty years as a school nurse, a field she never thought of pursuing. She came to the field totally by God's providence and over the years it has proven to be a significant source of funds for our children's education.

Started with dance …
*   fell in love with Greek and Latin*
Mary recalls the experience of our oldest daughter:

*   *   *

CHRISTINA'S EXPERIENCE WAS TRULY A GEM, AMONG MANY, OF
God supporting His child's education. Christina, our
second child, had her heart set on going to Columbia
University for undergraduate study, but had to give up
this idea and enroll in Brooklyn College. She started out
as a dance major but soon fell in love with the Greek
and Latin classics. She was always an excellent student
and finished at the top of her undergraduate class.

She then wanted to get a Ph.D. in Classics so that she
could teach. We thought that the best we could do was
to see if she could get into the least expensive graduate program in the public City University of New York
(CUNY). In order to be sure what the will of God was,
however, we also encouraged her to apply to Columbia
University, and Brown University in Rhode Island.
Both are well known for their programs in Classics. She
applied to all three schools — CUNY, Columbia, and
Brown — and we all prayed for a scholarship.

One evening, while we were together in our living
room, Christina received a phone call. A professor
from Columbia University asked if she could come to
Columbia for lunch the next day. He told her that she
was being considered for a scholarship but they wanted
to meet her first. She, of course, agreed to go and we all
rejoiced for this gift.

The next day she met with professors from the
Classics Department. She was offered a full tuition
scholarship and, in addition, a stipend of $10,000 per
year for her living expenses. After a few years, she also
taught a class which increased her stipend to $12,000
per year. Christina often felt that Providence gave

so much more than she needed to cover her living expenses while in graduate school. Once, for example, the family VCR player broke but we could not afford a replacement. Christina gave what she had extra to buy one for the family.

After seven years of study, she received her Ph.D. in Classics from Columbia University. She now teaches there as an adjunct.

*   *   *   *   *   *

Cash in hand

We felt strongly that at an early age each of our children should receive private music lessons to supplement what they learned at school. We wanted each child to take at least two years of private lessons on the piano, but we had no idea how we could pull this off. We did not own a piano and we didn't know how we could pay a music teacher. Then some unexpected things started happening.

When our first four children were still young, Tom's great-uncle Sig in Texas passed away and in his will he left us $900. "What a surprise!" we thought, "and what should we do with all that money?" It did not take long to agree that what the family needed most was a piano. Our friend Rob played quite well and had a very fine ear, so we asked him to help us find a second-hand piano. Together, we looked at lots of them. Finally we found one that sounded great and happened to match the maple finish and fluted legs of the furniture in our dining room, which we hoped would also serve as our music room. It seemed perfect in every way. The price, however, was $1,200. We told the owner that we needed a piano to start our children's lessons, but we had only $900 to spend. He said he could drop the price to an even $1,000 plus delivery charges. We didn't know what to do, except pray.

Immediately something came into Mary's mind that she didn't think was very important. "I don't know why I even said it, but I did." She told the man: "We have only the $900 in cash, and that's all we have." When the dealer heard "cash" his eyes lit up. Apparently most people paid him by check and a little at a time. After thinking a minute, he said, "I can give it to you for $900 in cash. I'll even give you a matching bench. And if we can close the deal today, I won't charge you for delivery."

That same afternoon, we had our very own piano. The lessons were made possible by Franca, one of our close friends who was an opera singer and a piano teacher. She had eleven children of her own and for a very low fee offered to teach our children two at a time. She also gave some of them voice lessons so that they could have small parts in the opera company she sang in.

We encouraged each of our children to take a minimum of two years of lessons so that they would learn the basics of music and to develop eye-hand coordination. They learned how to read music scores and to entertain each other — sometimes by playing duets of some classical pieces but mostly by playing the ragtime of Scott Joplin. We all loved to hear them played one after another, especially "Maple Leaf Rag" and "The Entertainer."

Most of the kids soon turned to other instruments. Many took up strings: guitars, both acoustic and electric; string bass, both acoustic and electric. One played the flute, another the clarinet, and another the violin. We had an oboe and bassoon player and, of course, a drummer. Ours was certainly never the quietest house on the block, and when the kids started jamming, we wondered why the windows did not blow out. Our neighbors must have loved music — even performed by young amateurs — because none of them ever complained.

When our eldest daughter got married, we had the reception in the house and the backyard. At one point the kids surprised the bride and groom with a concert of songs, some composed for the wedding itself. The guests squeezed together in our living room and overflowed onto the front porch. What Tolstoy said — "All art unites people" — was demonstrated that wedding day. From that point on such wedding concerts became a family tradition.

Something else helped us provide for our children's cultural education, especially in music and dance. When Tom's parents passed away, his portion of the inheritance amounted to $30,000. It seemed like an enormous sum, for that's exactly what we had paid for our house. This was our first opportunity to have some savings because up until then every penny we earned went for the daily needs of our large family. After looking at all the possibilities, we realized that we had nothing to give to the children for their education and might not ever be able to save anything, so we decided to divide the money and put it in a trust fund. In this way, when it was needed most each child would have $3,000 to use for education.

Since the money was in trust funds, the children could spend it only under our supervision. And they did use it wisely and in many different ways: to purchase guitars, a violin, a saxophone, to pay for dance lessons and gymnastic classes when family funds were lacking, to pay for the international youth festivals they were invited to attend in Europe. Many of them used their portion to learn new languages and new cultures by studying abroad for a summer, a semester, or a year.

With Providence, nothing is ever lacking!

Reflections

If we really believe that God is our "heavenly Father," as Jesus said he is, should we not trust that he will help us educate our children? If we really believe that God created our children with certain capabilities and talents, should we not trust that he will also give them opportunities to develop and perfect them through education? Jesus assures us, "Your heavenly Father knows that you need all these things. But strive first for the kingdom of God and his righteousness, and all these things will be given you as well. So do not worry …" (Mt 6:32–34).

What did Jesus mean when he said we have to "strive first for the kingdom of God and his righteousness"? How can we do this?

We might, for example, choose one main motive: "I do it for you, Lord, and for your kingdom." As we educate our children, as in everything we do, we can say in our hearts: "For you, Lord." This will remind us that our children are more God's than ours.

We also need to do God's will. When we do that we are already living in the kingdom of God on earth and are walking on the only sure road to the kingdom of God in heaven. Trying to do God's will as we educate our children will make us consider carefully the many things we have to do.

We have to help our children learn about the value of work by encouraging them to contribute to the cost of their tuition, so that they become co-responsible for their education. We ourselves have to save and sacrifice to help our children grow up to be mature adults. This means helping them learn how to live within their means as well as believing in Providence.

If we can manage to do so, we should have saving plans for their education. If we can't, we have to trust in his Providence. We should realize that living through the experiences of needing Providence helps children learn about the generosity of God and helps them set their priorities straight, so that they learn to "strive first for the kingdom of God."

Finally, we need to teach our children to work for God's righteousness, his justice, rather than their own, to prefer what he teaches in the scripture and in tradition rather than their own inclinations and feelings. This means to love all God's children — especially those persons who seem unlovable to us, those we might think are our enemies, for they are all loveable to our heavenly Father.

If we do these things ourselves, and teach our children to do them with us, we will see all the things we were worrying about fade away and all we desire for our children's education "will be given you as well. So do not worry."

Questions

1. How do children learn about Providence? How did you?
2. Whose obligation is it to educate children — parents, community, relatives, the government?
3. Can parents and grandparents model themselves after the first Christians who shared everything they had so that no one was in need?
4. Others depend on us to help them see Providence in action. How can we search our lives more for experiences that we can share?

5

Employment and Budgets

*Those who love God put Providence in their budgets;
they believe in the love of God for their families.*

Strangely beautiful . . . yet normal

We always found the task of making a family budget to be a huge challenge, although we fully understand the wisdom of doing so. It is one way of discovering God's will and God's love for our family. Tom once shared how he struggled with our budget.

* * *

I HAD BEEN PUTTING OFF WORKING OUT OUR FAMILY BUDGET FOR several reasons. First, I was pretty sure that our income was not enough to cover our expenses, and I was afraid to see how bad things really were. And then because we had twelve people in our family who all depended on my salary for survival, it made listing all the expenses for each month a rather complicated task.

But since I knew it was my responsibility to work out a budget, each time I put it off to do something I told myself was "more important," I felt more and more uneasy.

At a certain point, however, I began thinking more deeply about the will of God and particularly about listening to my inner voice in order to help me decide what

God wants for me in the present moment. One particular afternoon, I felt strongly urged to push all other matters aside for a few hours and focus on the family budget.

That night Mary had to attend a meeting, so after she left and I had put the children to bed, I cleared off the kitchen table and got out the paycheck stubs, the checkbook, and our little calculator. I then started listing all the bills that came in for the last few months in order to estimate our typical expenses for each month.

By the time Mary returned, I was nearly finished. She made us both a cup of tea and sat down at the table to review the figures together. We were both surprised to see that at the rate we were going, we would end up $300 short that month. We saw clearer than ever the impact of rising prices, especially for food and clothing. But we could not figure out a way to cut our expenses any further.

The only other alternative was to raise our income somehow. We talked about getting extra jobs, something we both have had to do in the past. But since our youngest was still not yet a year old, we decided that Mary should not return to work, even part time. I had already requested extra work, and the department chair had arranged for some for the following month. He also reminded me that I would be getting a little raise then too. But we still had no solution for the present month. We went to bed that night with an act of faith that God would provide.

The next morning I took all the little scraps of paper with my penciled figures on them and started typing up that month's budget into a neater form. Again I was struck by the harshness of the bottom line with its deficit of $300.

But as soon as I pulled the page from the typewriter, the phone rang. It was my department chair, calling to tell me about a new course that would be opening up next semester and to ask if I would like to teach it. This would not bring in any extra money, but it would leave me more time to spend with my family. Of course, I said yes. Then, almost as an afterthought, he mentioned that another teacher was in the hospital and would need someone to cover his classes. As if expecting me to say no, he asked if I could help him out for the rest of this month by taking one of the teacher's courses. He added that the extra pay I would get for this would be at least $300.

Once again I learned that trying to discern what God wants brings incredible results. As I hung up the phone, my spine was tingling and my mind was racing: "How strange! How strangely beautiful! And, yet, in a way, how normal." Divine Providence is not an abstract concept. God is not a distant philanthropist looking down on us from another dimension. Divine Providence is a father, my father, who is here and who loves me in a personal way.

* * *   * * *

At a seminar for families Mary related this story from her own work life:

* * *

WE HAVE TEN CHILDREN AND MY MOTHER ALSO LIVES WITH US. IN all the years of trying to raise our large family, we've always believed that God loves us immensely. We have often experienced his great and concrete love for us through the providence that he constantly and generously sends our way.

I'm a registered nurse. Four years ago, when our youngest child was three years old, we thought that it was time for me to go back to work to help meet our family's financial needs, which had increased at that time because we had children in college.

A refresher course with "flexible hours"

I had not worked in the nursing field for almost eighteen years. Even though I did keep up with nursing trends and practice through professional journals, I thought I would not be able to get a job without taking a refresher course, but that would be costly and take a lot of time. Because we still had young school-age children, I could work only part-time and only during hours that coincided with the children's school schedule. But I also thought that if my going back to work was part of what God wanted for me and for our family, his Providence would present itself in the form of a job.

One afternoon, as I was sitting on my front porch watching the children play, my next-door neighbor came over to ask if I would be interested in working as a school nurse. A part-time position was open at the school for the deaf where she worked. I was a pediatric nurse but I never ever thought of school nursing or working with children with disabilities. It was clear to me that through my neighbor's request, God was helping me find a way to get back into the profession that I loved so much and that I had willingly put aside to care for our family.

I made an appointment for the interview. As I prepared for it, I felt urged to figure out the actual hours I could devote to working. Since being present for our children was my top priority, I studied their school's schedules carefully. Then I wrote my possible work hours on an index card. When I met with the principal of the school for my interview, she seemed eager to offer me the job and I was excited at the possibility of being a practicing nurse again. However, I couldn't take the position without the "flexible hours" that I had determined the day before. So, at a certain point, I handed her my index card. She was so surprised! She said, "I'm not sure about this. I'll have to think about it. I'll call you tomorrow." She did call the next day to say she would hire me for the exact hours noted on my card. And of course I accepted. This job proved to be a very practical gift of Providence, a true hundredfold, because I worked with a seasoned school nurse who taught me everything I needed to know about school nursing. This was surely God's version of a refresher course that gave me a secure footing back into my field without compromising the care of our family. I was even paid for it!

Knowing how much … would help

A year later, we examined our finances again and found that, in spite of my additional earnings, we were still not covering all our expenses. What else could we do? Scripture tells us, "Ask and you shall receive, seek and you shall find." But, we thought, maybe knowing how much to ask for would help. So we sat down to work out an annual budget that included our family's every need, from maintenance of the house, education, and medical costs to our family's summer vacation and spiritual retreats for all of us. Clearly, my salary was not helping as much as we thought. As a remedy, we decided to ask God for another job for me, one that would match our needs. We put everything in God's hands.

Shortly after, I responded to an ad in the newspaper for a part-time school nurse position. When the interviewer asked for my salary requirements, I told him with confidence, $20,000, the exact amount we needed. I also mentioned my available work hours and handed him my index card. He seemed a little surprised and I could see that he was working out the figures in his head. Then he said, "I think what you're asking for is even a little low for a nurse with your experience but frankly, it's what we can afford for now since the school is just opening and our budget is a little tight." And so my next adventure as a school nurse started.

Replacing God with another god

The school year passed quickly and I was off for the summer. When I returned to work in the Fall, I received the news that due to budget cuts, the state eliminated the nurse's position for this school. What a huge disappointment! This meant that I had to look for another job. This time though, I felt that something in me had changed. I was now used to earning a certain amount of money and we were a little more comfortable financially. I was more concerned about just getting any job that would continue providing us with our newly found financial "comfort." I started working at a home care agency further away from our home. I had to trade my "flexible hours" for longer hours, which meant less availability for our family. I would leave at eight in the morning and not return until six in the evening four days every week. Since it was more stressful, I was exhausted and unable to really care for the family when I returned home from work. Without realizing it, I had replaced God with another god.

I remember arriving at work one day, struggling with myself and questioning why I was doing what I was doing. The care of the children had always been a priority for me and I understood a long time ago that God had entrusted them to me. I felt far from the will of God and I searched within to discover why I felt this way. The answer came to me: I no longer relied on God's Providence but on my own self, and I was not happy. That answer again brought to light God's immense love for me; I decided to let go of everything immediately to get back on track.

I spoke to my boss and told him that I couldn't continue working for the agency because I needed more time to be with my family. He listened and then said, "Why don't you work as a consultant? That way, you can continue doing our staff training." This unexpected response from him caught me by surprise. "You can set your hourly fee and decide how many hours you want to work," he said. I never thought of working as a consultant. Another encouragement from Providence! So I became a nurse consultant. I established an hourly fee and decreased my work days and hours. I was there again for our family. And Tom and I were amazed to find that my earnings as a consultant were not much less than what I received as a salaried employee for this agency.

I discovered again that if I try to do the will of God, he always shows me a better — and often unexpected — way.

*   *   *   *   *   *

Reflections

The poets of the Romantic period were sensitive to how Providence governs the movements of the universe and to how secular society draws people away from an awareness of "the ways of God" in their lives. We can be so preoccupied with working and accumulating wealth and shopping for more and more things that we leave little or no time for appreciating nature and being grateful for the gifts that come from God. William Wordsworth expressed it bluntly yet beautifully in these lines taken from one of his sonnets:

> *The world is too much with us; late and soon,*
> *Getting and spending, we lay waste our powers:*
> *Little we see in Nature that is ours;*
> *We have given our hearts away, a sordid boon!*

The constant bombardment of television and radio advertisements provokes our eyes and ears with temptations to shape our lives around "getting and spending." People spend their days off in shopping malls, and take walks there even on sunny days. Some call it "window shopping" and admit they go "just to check out the best prices." Where we spend our free time can give a good indication of what we value most in life.

Since life is short and people are more valuable than things, Wordsworth can rightly claim that by placing a high priority on shopping for things we "waste our powers," making us victims of consumerism. On the contrary, if we use our powers for people, helping those who need our help, we will "show the heavens more just."

One practical way of collaborating with God and using the gifts he has lavished on us is to make an annual comprehensive budget. This budget should include all our incomes, our basic needs, and what our family will need that might not be covered by our incomes, such as travel for education, musical instruments, family vacations, and the needs of others. If we work as collaborators with God in this way, we will also be thanking God for giving us all the powers we have.

Questions

1. How do you deal with the pull toward "getting and spending"?
2. Have you ever felt that God intervened to help with your financial needs?
3. How does God's Providence relate to your line of work or profession?
4. Do you make a budget? Does it include Providence?

6

Paying Taxes and Planning Retirement

Give to Caesar what belongs to Caesar,
and to God what belongs to God.

MT 22:21

Not long ago we attended a meeting for couples who were trying to help each other put the gospel into their daily lives. They did this most effectively by sharing their own experiences of how they were able to do it or how they failed and had to struggle to start again. These meetings helped us all not to be discouraged, and sometimes they were quite inspiring. Most of all, they were practical.

You know what we need ... by April 15

One particular meeting focused on the place of prayer in our lives. After some people talked, there was a quiet moment. Tom felt that he should say something, but as he searched his memory he could come up with nothing that seemed worth saying. As the silence lasted longer and longer, Tom started to pray to the Holy Spirit to help him think of something that would be good for these particular people. The man sitting next to him kept moving uneasily in his chair when people spoke — looking not at them, but at the floor, at the ceiling — apparently wishing he could be somewhere

else. He seemed worried. Tom asked the Holy Spirit
again for help and this is what came out:

*   *   *

SOME YEARS AGO, MARY AND I FIGURED OUT OUR TAXES AS WE
usually did at the end of February. We always did them
as early as possible so that our tax refunds, which were
substantial because of our large family, would come
back sooner. This time, however, we were shocked to
discover that we owed the government $900. It was
a shock because every year before we got refunds of
about the same amount. At that time we lived literally
from paycheck to paycheck and had no savings. We
were really getting worried because we didn't know
what to do.

We decided to go to the Newman Center chapel nearby
and pray together in front of the Eucharist for what we
needed. Since the chapel was empty we sat down next to
each other in front of the tabernacle and said something
like this: "You are God, so you know what we need. You
gave us many children and we always trusted that you
would help us take care of them. They are your children
more than ours. We need your help now. Next month,
on April 15, we need exactly $900." Right away we felt
peaceful. We got up and went back home.

The following week the dean at my school asked
if I could go to Bridgeport, Connecticut, to speak to
teachers there about what we had been doing at our
school for faculty development and curricular development. I had been helping the dean with these projects
for several years, but up until now she had made all the
speeches and I stayed in the background. Because I had

never done anything like that before, I was reluctant to accept her offer. Just thinking about it made me nervous. She said that the stipend would be $250. What immediately flashed through my mind was, "This is God's first installment on the tax bill," so I accepted.

Then Mary was asked if she could present a workshop on homeopathy and first-aid for parents. One of our doctors had been encouraging her to do this for a long time because there was such a need for it. Up until then, Mary thought she would have to find a large classroom to use since no room in our house was big enough. It also seemed impossible to teach at home with all the kids around. Still, we felt that we had to do something, so we decided that one Saturday I would take all the children out for the day and Mary would set up the living room as a classroom. She managed to do a whole-day program for parents, who came from near and far upon recommendations from their doctors. This installment amounted to another $200.

I was asked to give another talk at another school and was paid $150, and then we got another $50 from a source I can't remember. In any event, I remember most vividly, as if it were yesterday, that three days before April 15 we had a total of $600. Even though we still needed $300, God was doing such a great job with his surprises up to that point that we were confident he would not stop now.

We prayed a lot that night and the next day, and sometimes started to doubt and worry, but we kept on praying. On April 14, we picked up our mail from the front porch. In the pile was an envelope with the return address of an old friend who had moved to Canada and had not written in years. When we were students we were close, and met with a few others every week in my apartment to discuss art and philosophy. We had some great arguments about aesthetics, for we each had different views of what constitutes beauty. Those memories flashed through my mind as I opened the envelope and found this short note:

> *Dear Tom,*
> *I'm doing well, but I feel that you and Mary may*
> *need some help right now.*
> > *Love to you both,*
> > *Pat*

Inside the envelope was his check for $300.

*   *   *   *   *   *

While Tom was sharing this experience, Mary noticed that the man next to him had stopped fidgeting and looking around the room, and fixed his eyes on Tom. He sat up straight as if totally wrapped up in the story. Afterwards his wife told Mary that her husband recently started his own business and was struggling to find ways to pay his taxes. We realized that our experience in trusting in Providence was not for us alone but a gift to be shared with those who need it as much as we did. And the Holy Spirit would tell us when to do it.

Retirement and inheritance

Tom's relatives and colleagues and friends often ask about his plans for retirement and for leaving something for our children when we pass on. We have thought about this quite a lot, and here is the way Tom summed it up:

* * *

IN ADDITION TO THE BURDENS AND JOYS OF TAKING CARE OF OUR own ten children and many of Mary's relatives, we frequently had to take care of our children's friends and other kids as well. One high school girl came to us when a nun asked us to take the girl in because her violent father threw her out. She had no place else to go. Some kids came to dinner, some stayed overnight, some stayed on for weeks, and a few — like that high school girl — stayed for months. Some who had come from other countries could not find work right away to support themselves. Most of these kids could not get help from their own parents and so they adopted us.

Because of all these wonderful people, whose extended visits brought us many headaches but many more happy moments, we found it was impossible to save anything. So we had to deal with more questions that were often put to us: What will you live on in your old age? How many IRA's and investments do you have to rely on for income? We are also often asked, "What will you leave to your children? Will they have any inheritance?

God seems to be solving these problems for us. His Providence keeps working day and night.

As far as support for our later years, we discovered that my pension turned out to be more than satisfactory for our basic needs. When added to Social Security it is almost equal to my salary when I was working. This is true even though we chose to have the pension reduced so that it would not only cover me for the rest of my life but also cover Mary for the rest of her life if she outlives me. So that solved the problem of not saving up for our old age.

*   *   *   *   *   *

As for leaving some kind of inheritance for our children, we are finding that we have two things we never thought much about:

First, the big old Victorian house we bought over forty years ago for $30,000 when we were newlyweds has been increasing in value every year. We heard that it is now worth over thirty times as much as we paid for it. We plan to leave that to the children through a trust fund.

Second, we really believe that the most important things we can leave to our children will not be the old house and a couple of insurance policies, but some things that are hard to measure and easy to forget. They are hard to see and even harder to talk about. We mean our way of living, our ideals, our teachings about relationships and suffering and loving — all those gifts of the Holy Spirit that we received from Chiara Lubich and the spirituality of unity, which we have tried to pass on to our children. We hope that these gifts of God will be the real inheritance that we leave to our children and our grandchildren, and that they will treasure them above all.

Reflections

A lot depends on how we look at our possessions. Do we feel we have absolute ownership of them, or are we simply administrators of what God has given us and what he wants us to use as we live out his commandment to love one another? If we make the right choice perhaps each of us can begin to solve the inequality among peoples by sharing more and cooperating with Divine Providence.

In some countries with an abundance of wealth, many are plagued by consumerism, while other countries have so little wealth and so few resources that most of their people cannot fill their basic needs. To discover "a remedy" for this "tragic inequality" Chiara Lubich directs us to a scripture passage:

> "Give and gifts will be given to you; a good measure, packed together, shaken down, and overflowing, will be poured into your lap" (Lk 6:38). To give, to give; to make our giving real. To give rise to and foster a culture of giving.
>
> Let's give the extra we have or even what is necessary if that's what our heart suggests to us; to give to those in need, knowing full well that this way of using our things yields unlimited interest because our giving opens God's hands and he, in his Providence, fills us overabundantly so that we can give even more and in even greater amounts, and then receive again and thus help meet the endless needs of many, many others.[1]

When a group of teenagers asked her to explain what she meant by a "culture of giving," Lubich gave a clear and simple answer:

---

1. Telephone Conference Call message, April 23, 1992.

You should keep for yourself only what you need: like plants do. They absorb from the earth only the water, minerals and other things they need and no more. All the rest should be given away and shared with others.[2]

Moreover, she proposed "the culture of giving" as "the perfect antidote to the affliction of consumerism."

Questions

1. What do you think Jesus meant when he said, "Give to Caesar what belongs to Caesar and to God what belongs to God"?
2. "Giving opens God's hands." What does this mean to you?
3. What does a "culture of giving" mean to you? What is its opposite?
4. Have you experienced unfairness in your life?
5. What do you plan to do when you retire?

---

2. Youth Convention ("Supercongress"), Marino, Italy, June 12, 1992.

7

Providence Overflowing to Others

"Love goes around the world."

W hen we traveled to New Zealand for our oldest son's wedding, we got quite a surprise. In
his speech at the reception, the best man told everyone how he met our family some years earlier when
he passed through New York. We had not seen him
for many years because he got married and settled in
Australia. He spoke highly of our son and our family
and mentioned something we had totally forgotten.
During the few days he spent with us in New York, he
went down in the basement to do his laundry. When he
went down to unload it and put it in the dryer, however,
he found the whole load was all white — blotchy white.
All his clothes were ruined because instead of liquid
soap he had poured in liquid bleach.

After we all had lots of laughs, Mary took him out
to buy new clothes, because he had little money of his
own. He saw this as a gift of Providence and we did too,
although we don't recall where the money came from.

His joy was multiplied … a hundredfold

Over the years, we have had many experiences
of receiving Providence and of being the source of
Providence for others. We always marvel at the hundredfold that was never lacking. Mary recalls one of
these precious moments of Providence having to do

with a choice that our son Peter made when he was only seven or eight years old:

*   *   *

ON OUR GRANDSON LEO'S TENTH BIRTHDAY WE WANTED TO GIVE him a gift. We had been quite busy, however, so we didn't have time to shop. Tom and I agreed that it was best to give him some money. I mentioned this to his mother, Christina, who also agreed. So I went to give Leo twenty dollars. As I was handing him the money, some thoughts flashed through my mind about our son Peter when he was a little younger than Leo.

On his seventh or eighth birthday, Peter decided that he wanted to share the money that he received as gifts for his birthday with his five brothers and sisters. Peter thought that it would be great if we all went to a toy store not only to buy something for him, but to let his brothers and sisters choose a gift for themselves. Touched by his generosity, we encouraged him even though we wondered how he was going to buy some-thing for each of them, since he did not have much money in hand. We were concerned about disappoint-ing the children and thought, "Maybe we'll just have to cover whatever he can't."

However, as the six of them went around the store looking at one toy or another, with the help of his older siblings who got really involved, Peter himself figured out the cost of each item including the tax. He made sure that they did not spend more than he had. Each of them was ready to choose an item that cost less, even letting go of something they really would like to have gotten, so that no one would go without. Peter was visibly happy in sharing his gift money and his joy was multiplied as he saw the others so happy as well.

There was a lot of chatter in the car on our way home, and when we arrived, they experienced the hundredfold of playing with each other's toys. It was quite moving to watch them.

And so, after a moment of surprise at Peter's experience re-emerging in my mind, I handed Leo his twenty dollars. As I did so, I told him, "Leo, Grandpapa and I would like you to buy a birthday gift for yourself and maybe celebrate with your brother and sisters by sharing this with them too." Right away he said, "O.K. That's a great idea, Grammy!" When he called later to tell us how things went, we could hear the same joy in his voice that we heard years earlier from our children. Leo's mom reported later that her other three children also understood what Leo had done. They were more open to sharing with each other, and were happy when their siblings joined in as they celebrated the next two birthdays in the same way.

We were thrilled to know Peter's idea of giving has been taken up by the next generation.

* * * * * *

Practically blind without them

A friend of our daughter Christina, a graduate student, had been staying with us for a few months. One day, his eyeglasses broke. He was practically blind without them. We were sitting at the kitchen table as he lamented the loss of his glasses; without them he could not study. We turned to him and said, "Would you like us to take you to get new glasses?" He answered, "Yes, but I don't have money to pay for them right now." We had the same thought — that we didn't have money to pay for them either. The only way we could have paid for them was by credit card. Although we usually tried to avoid using credit, in this instance, it seemed right to take a risk out of love. So, without hesitating, we said, "Let's go get your glasses." He was very grateful and promised to find a way to pay us back. Shortly after, when he was asked by a friend to help paint a few rooms in the house across the street, he earned enough to reimburse us. The temporary investment in those glasses paid off. He is now a university professor and has a family of his own. Although we don't see each other often, our relationship remains.

Adopting at a distance

Love really does extend clear around the world! Mary explains a particular way that our family experienced this:

*   *   *

IN THE EARLY 80S, WE FIRST HEARD ABOUT "ADOPTION AT A Distance," one of the many socio-economic development projects that the Focolare's New Humanity Movement sponsors around the world, particularly in underdeveloped countries. Adoption at a Distance provides education, nutrition, and healthcare for children as well as skills training programs and employment for their parents, so families can remain intact.

Unlike programs that remove children from the direct care of their families, Adoption at a Distance provides assistance to families so that children can remain in the care of their parents. This project does not offer the poor a "handout." Instead, it proceeds from the idea that because the poor are our brothers and sisters they are members of our family. Those who offer children regular financial support do so from a distance. Parents and children are not separated, and families maintain their human dignity, while remaining immersed in their culture and connected within the very fabric of their society.

At the time, we had eight children and we were also supporting my mom and sister who had come from the Philippines to live with us. At first we felt that we did not have the means to adopt a child, although we really wanted to. My heart was deeply moved because before coming to the United States I too was one of those "poor children." Although we now had a big family to support, we had everything we needed and we were never hungry. Tom and I also thought that it would be really good to encourage our children to live for others, including those who are far away from us and not our relatives.

One day, an idea came to us. We gathered the children together and told them about Adoption at a Distance. We also told them that if they agreed, we could all adopt a child together for $180 each year. The children thought this was a great idea too. But where would we find $180?

In those days, we used to order pizza once a week as a treat and also to give me and the children a free night from cooking. As we talked together, we figured out that if we skipped just one week's pizza each month, we could easily come up with the $180 that we needed to support a child. We decided to go ahead with this plan.

We were assigned an adopted child through a New Humanity project in the Philippines called *Bukas Palad* (Open Palm of the Hands). We were all excited when a letter arrived from Jeffrey, a young boy who lived with

his mother near the *Bukas Palad* school in a suburb of
Manila. Twice a year his joyful letters let us know how
he was doing in school. His family eventually moved
away from *Bukas Palad* and we lost contact with Jeffrey.
Then we were introduced to Philip, a young boy with a
physical handicap who lived with his mother and sister.
For many years, he too wrote faithfully; we still have his
picture, with his beautiful smile, in our dining room.

Although some donors have gone to visit their
adopted children and their families, we never had the
opportunity to meet Jeffrey or Philip in person. Still,
we felt privileged to have been a small part of these
children's lives.

And we didn't miss the pizzas either.

*   *   *   *   *   *

"I would like to help too — and I think I can."

Some years ago Tom wrote this experience concern-
ing how the reach of our family's love has extended
around the world:

*   *   *

SHORTLY AFTER I MET THE FOCOLARE I WENT TO LEARN MORE
about it at the Movement's center in Italy. There I met
many people from different nations, among them a
man from Brazil who translated for me. During our
two weeks together we became real friends. He told
me about the trials of his six-year-old daughter, who
was born with spina bifida, a condition in which the
lower part of her spine does not completely enclose
the spinal cord. An operation to close the opening and

protect the nerves failed, causing paralysis from the waist down. When she reached school age, her mother had to accompany her, because she was incontinent and needed someone to change her diapers regularly.

My friend said he heard that in the United States it was possible to purchase a bag that could be strapped onto the leg to collect urine. With such a device he hoped his daughter could attend school on her own and avoid the social embarrassment of wearing diapers. I assured him that if such a device was available I would try to get one for his daughter.

After I returned I asked several doctors I know to help me find the urinary bag so I could send it to my friend in Brazil. But when they looked into the matter, they found that no such device was ever found to work for women, especially for little girls. They discovered that the devices either leaked, or the necessary adhesive irritated the skin and led to infections.

This was a big disappointment, because I felt I had to tell my friend that I could not help his little girl. Although I had done my part and was told that there was nothing more that I could do, I still did not feel at peace.

Before I had a chance to write, a businessman arrived from Brazil with a message from him. He gave me specific instructions about where I might purchase the urinary bag in New York City, complete with catalogue descriptions and photos. Given what I'd already found out, I suspected that this search would be most likely a waste of time. Nevertheless, I wanted to love my friend all the way to the end.

So, at my first opportunity to take off from work, I jumped on the subway and went to the offices of a large medical supply company in downtown Manhattan. I told the receptionist that I needed some equipment for a person in Brazil. She immediately called for the executive in charge of their South American accounts. I guess she thought I was a purchasing agent or somebody important enough to place a big order.

Soon an elegantly dressed lady who was originally from Colombia came to help me. Right away I told her that I did not represent a company but merely had come to seek help for my Brazilian friend's daughter, whose problem I explained briefly. I think she understood that my motivations were completely selfless. She gave me her full attention and then started looking through catalogues to find out where the bags were produced. She explained that her company found that they did not work well and had stopped distributing them.

My telling her how sorry I was to take so much of her time seemed to make her even more eager to help. Even when other clients interrupted our conversation, she asked them to wait, just as if she were with a major client. She even went so far as to telephone manufacturers throughout the country in order to make sure we checked out all the latest devices on the market. After almost an hour in her office, we had to conclude that the advice of my doctor friends was quite correct. There was no available urinary bag for a six-year-old girl. Even though I was disappointed, I was deeply impressed by the care and kindness that this sales manager had extended to me.

Just before I left, she gave me a list of other medical supply stores and suggested I consult them on the chance that they could suggest other options. I felt this would be rather futile, but to show my thankfulness to

her and to love my friend to the end, I said I would
try them all. So I took the subway uptown and started
walking from one medical supply store to another. The
clerks all said basically the same thing: what I was looking for was not available. It was afternoon by the time I
left the last store, and I felt that I probably should give
up and go back home. Since I hadn't brought a lunch
and had only one subway token left in my pocket, head-
ing home seemed to be the right thing to do. I had done
my part. I could not be expected to do more.

And still I was not completely at peace — and that
made me wonder whether I was really doing the will
of God. The image of my Brazilian friend asking me
to help his little girl and my assuring him that I would
do whatever I could kept coming back to my mind. A
little voice inside of me suggested that I should keep
searching for an answer. I felt that this huge city — with
all its research hospitals — had to contain at least one
scientist who could help us.

As soon as I decided to continue my search, I remembered something: one of the clerks I had talked to earlier
said that New York Hospital did a lot of research on
children's health problems. I kept telling myself, "Keep
loving to the end, even if it takes all afternoon." So I
walked the mile or so to New York Hospital, where I
was told that all the doctors were out to lunch until two
o'clock. Since I had no money for lunch, I took a long
drink from the water fountain and went to the medical
library to read. While sitting there, I remembered what
Jesus said about being as clever as foxes, so I made a little
plan of how I would get to talk with the right doctors.

So when two o'clock came, I went straight to the person in charge, asking the receptionist to telephone the

head of the Department of Urology. I told his secretary that I was "Dr. Hartmann" and wanted the advice of the department head about who could help me with a complicated case of a paralyzed and incontinent child. She didn't ask me what kind of doctor I was, and I didn't let on that I was not a specialist in urology but in English poetry. The secretary said that since the head urologist was not back yet, she would transfer me to the specialists in pediatric urology. "The office of the Head of Urology referred me to you," I told the first doctor I reached. And then I explained the problem. He said he was happy to say that on the ninth floor of New York Hospital there was a doctor doing research precisely on this kind of patient and that if anyone could help me he could. He switched me to the researcher's office and I spoke to his secretary: "I am Dr. Hartmann. I am downstairs and need to consult with the research doctor about an important case in Brazil that would interest him." She said, "Come up right away. I'll tell him you're coming."

When I got to his office, I prayed to the Holy Spirit that I would say the right things. I knew then that above all I had to love this doctor with all my might, and this meant telling him the full truth right away. As soon as I walked into his office, I confessed that I was Dr. Hartmann, an English professor trying to help a friend whom I met in Italy a few months earlier. He was very gracious and listened to the whole story of the little girl's troubles and my futile attempts to find a urinary bag for her.

After asking a few questions, he surprised me by saying, "It's admirable what you are doing for this family, and I would like to help too — and I think I can." He then explained that urinary bags are really not the answer and that his research had found that drugs and catheters can be used to control the bladders of children so that they can attend school in a somewhat normal way. In fact, a number of children even younger had been using his system for years with great success. Then he said that there was a doctor in Brazil about to start using his therapy there, and he gave me his address. He also said, however, that he would prefer to have my friend bring his daughter from Brazil to New York so that he could examine her himself and make sure she got the right drugs for her problem. I told him there was hardly any chance of that since the family was not well off, but before leaving I promised to invite them to New York. Perhaps, I thought, some miracle of Providence would bring them here.

That evening I returned home hungry and very tired — but full of joy. My little acts of love were returned that day in surprising ways by almost every person I met, especially the South American sales executive and the doctor at New York Hospital. I felt I had done my part to love to the end. For the first time that day, I felt completely at peace.

But that's not the end of the story. After he received my letter, my friend brought his daughter right away to the Brazilian doctor that had been recommended to me. Unfortunately, he did not get much help because the research in Sao Paolo was not as advanced as it was in New York. Then, a few months later, I got a letter that was full of surprises. My friend asked me to set up an appointment for his daughter at New York Hospital during the last week of May. Through a series of what can only be called miracles, they found a way to come to the United States. Only after they arrived did I hear the full story.

First, my friend's wife was invited to attend a Focolare festival for families in Rome in early May. Then, my friend himself was asked to help plan a tour for the one hundred Brazilians and one hundred Argentineans going to the FamilyFest and to accompany them as a guide throughout Italy, for he not only knew the country but also spoke Portuguese, Spanish, and Italian. They were both able to get tickets from Sao Paolo to Rome with a stopover in New York.

The only remaining problem was paying for their daughter's ticket. As the time grew short, they went to the airline and explained their need to bring their daughter with them on their trip. They asked if there was some kind of special discount or financial aid. The airline official gave them a big smile and said, "No problem, for this is the 'Year of the Handicapped.' All handicapped passengers go free on our airline this whole year." When I heard this, I wept with joy and felt that a tiny act of love on my part was snowballing into an amazing series of events that appeared no less than miraculous.

When the Brazilian family finally did arrive in New York, many other families shared with us the responsibility of taking care of them during the week they spent here. For my family, their presence here was an extraordinary gift, and their child was a continual source of joy for all of us, especially for my children.

Shortly before they left, the father sat in our kitchen with tears flowing down his cheeks as he described their days in the hospital and their long consultations with "the brilliant and most kind doctor" who had arranged that they would not be charged a single penny. He also spoke of their contacts with families here, and I'll never forget his last words to me: "No human family could accomplish what was done here. Not only did I get more help for my daughter than I ever expected, but the love of everyone involved made me feel that my family really extends around the whole world."

This experience made me realize many things, but the greatest is that we never know what amazing consequences may follow from even small acts of love. When we love, we participate in the actions of God, and acts of God always reach far beyond human expectations, sometimes revealing things that seem more divine than human. I realized, more than ever before, how much God loves us and how much we need to believe in his Providence.

*   *   *   *   *   *

Reflections

We are one human family with each member deserving the love and care fitting a child of God. The early Christians set a wonderful example of taking care of each other: "There was not a needy person among them" (Acts 4:34). It's enough to look around where we live and look at the nightly news on TV to know that this is one of our great challenges today: "not a needy person among them." We are all called to meet this challenge. If we're attentive to the promptings of Divine Providence, we can accomplish this task in creative and innovative ways.

Chiara Lubich had a genius for coming up with new ideas and for putting these ideas into action. Adoption at a Distance, which is mentioned in this chapter, is just

one of her many ideas that have succeeded in changing
societies around the world.

There is another project that has begun to have an
impact on a global scale in economic theory and business practices: the Economy of Communion, popularly
known as the "EoC." When Chiara Lubich visited Brazil
in 1991, she was struck by the extremes of poverty in
the midst of wealth there, and so she created a plan
for a new kind of economy that is intended to bridge
the chasm between the rich and poor. She encouraged
Focolare communities to establish businesses in a new
way that is rooted in the gospel, thus preserving the dignity of both those who have and those who have not.
Dr. Lorna Gold has summarized the essential elements:

> The novelty of the project was initially seen as
> the division of the profits of the businesses
> into three parts.... One part was to be given
> to the poor, one kept for re-investment in the
> firm and the third part for the creation of edu-
> cational structures to promote the "culture of
> giving."
>
> (NEW FINANCIAL HORIZONS 88–89)

When Chiara Lubich was awarded an honorary doc-
torate in economics in 1999, she emphasized another
aspect of the EoC:

> We must not forget, however, another essential
> element: Providence. It has constantly accom-
> panied the development of the Economy of
> Communion throughout the years. Space
> is left in the enterprises of the Economy of

Communion for God's intervention even
within the hard facts of economic reality.

(ESSENTIAL WRITINGS 277)

She noted, for example, that when EoC business
leaders followed their ideals and went against the cur-
rent of common business practices, Providence never
failed to intervene. Unexpected revenue, ideas for new
products confirmed that they were on the right track.

Adoption at a Distance and the Economy of
Communion are two major contributions to building
up a new culture, a "culture of giving" that is helping in
practical ways to reduce the gap between the rich and
the poor.

Questions

1. How do you view those who are rich and those
   who are poor?
2. What can you do to bridge the gap between rich
   and poor?
3. What charitable activities can you participate in
   to work together with the poor in your neighborhood or city?
4. What can you do about the suffering of people in
   other countries?

8

When Providence Fails

Trust the past to the mercy of God, the present to his love, and the future to his Providence.

SAINT AUGUSTINE

A s the first eight chapters have demonstrated, trusting in God and relying on his Providence has become our normal way of life. Nevertheless, as we look back on our family's experience, we do recall moments of darkness when we thought God had failed to help us.

How can anyone do this to us?

In Chapter 2, we shared the experience of buying what we thought was a second-hand Dodge station wagon. It turned out that the seller was a front man for a gang that fleeced unsuspecting customers by turning back the odometers of older cars to make them look as if they had not been driven much. Detectives told us that we were only one victim of many who had been hoodwinked. Some of the gang had been arrested. If we wanted to recover what we paid for the car, we would have to wait until they had been convicted and then go to court and sue them. When we heard this, our hearts dropped. We had six children and so little money then that the loss really hurt. It was terribly unfair. How could anyone do this to us? We really were fooled by that "nice man" — and right in front of his wife and kids and ours too! How could we have been so stupid?

We felt that this time Providence had failed us, and we went through a dark period. We could see no light at all, but we did not despair. We may not have had much hope, but we did have a lot of faith. We prayed and prayed that God would help us find a car that would be big enough for our six children and us. We also prayed that somehow we'd end up with an honest deal and a safe car.

And sure enough, God's generous Providence appeared through our elderly neighbors, who surprised us with the money for a brand new nine-passenger station wagon.

Often God seems to fail us because we are too short sighted—we focus on immediate results and are too impatient to wait to see the whole picture. This happened to us a number of times.

In the middle of nowhere

One summer the New York area beaches were closed for health reasons — medical waste was discovered along all our shores. So we decided to investigate taking our vacation up north in Canada, where the beaches were reported to be clean and safe.

When we told the children they got excited because for some time they had been poring over the books of the Canadian writer L. M. Montgomery and had been watching faithfully all the enactments of her stories in the TV series "Anne of Green Gables," set on a Canadian island with the natural beauty of paradise and whose characters had the winning simplicity and purity of farm folk. Both the setting and the little dramas fascinated all of our children. They said they were dying to see the real place where the author lived and the beautiful country and people she lived with.

The place was called Prince Edward Island and we discovered that it had lots of things that attracted us all. It really was an island separated from the mainland of Canada. We would have to travel there in a big ship, which would take over an hour to cross the sea. We'd even be able to put our car on the ship. To our city kids, this sounded much more exciting than taking our little Staten Island Ferry.

Equally exciting was the thought of living for a couple of weeks in a big old farmhouse on a real working farm with cows and horses and tractors, and of course chickens running all over the place. What's more, the farm was located only a half-hour drive from many beaches, beaches free of the pollution that plagued New York City, beaches with miles of sand that stretched from right to left as far as one could see. We were told that there would be few people there. We certainly would find none of the crowds we were used to at Coney Island or Jones Beach.

The more we studied Prince Edward Island, the more we felt it was the perfect place for our vacation, so we made our reservations for the ship and for rooms at the farm — with meals included. As soon as school ended, we packed our van and headed north.

Our plan was to drive straight up through Maine, make a quick stop at Acadia National Park, and then continue on to Canada. Before we reached Acadia, however, our van broke down and had to be towed to a garage. Tom went with the tow truck while Mary and the kids got a lift to a nearby motel. When Tom joined them in the evening, he had to report that the engine needed a rare part and that it might take several days before it could be found.

Every one of us was deeply disappointed. Here we were wasting the first days of our precious vacation in a small motel room in a small town in the middle of nowhere with nothing to do but wait, for who knows how long, for our car to be repaired. It bothered Mary and Tom that they would have to spend some of the money saved for the vacation on the motel and the car repairs, not to mention perhaps losing days at the farm, which had been paid for in advance. It bothered the children that they had to set aside their dreams and had to sit and wait, abandoned in the middle of nowhere. We all felt a big letdown and repeated: "What a way to begin our summer vacation!" Even God seemed to have forgotten us. Was he perhaps too far away to see our trouble? Did he not hear our prayers?

The next day we started to investigate that very quiet, rural part of Maine. Someone told us that the state fair was taking place not too far away — in fact, within walking distance. Since we could find nothing better for all of us to do together, we decided to take a walk to the fairgrounds to see if anything was interesting. We were surprised. There was something for everyone, especially the children.

For city kids like ours, their first experience of a state fair was eye popping because everything was so different from anything they had seen before. There were rides and games and cotton candy. We all had so much fun that we almost forgot about our broken-down van. We were beginning to see that Providence had a plan that was somewhat different from the one we had made. And we were learning to be more and more trusting in what he had planned for us.

When we got back to the motel and called the auto shop we got another surprise. The mechanic found the part he needed and the van was ready to be picked up. The next morning we were back on the road, admiring the spectacular views of forest and mountain and sea-side in Acadia National Park. Although we didn't have time to stop, we didn't mind at all because the children were dying to get to the ship that would take us to the farmhouse on Prince Edward Island. And it was all that we imagined: a little bit of paradise.

I was really fired

Providence seemed to have failed us on another occasion, when Tom was fired from his college teaching job. He will tell what happened:

* * *

I WAS STILL YOUNG, AN ASSISTANT PROFESSOR IN THE DEPART-ment of English, when I was invited to teach in a special program to help adult students get through the first years of college quickly even while they were working full-time. It was a prestigious assignment; some even called it "cushy" because it involved teaching only one class with only twenty-five carefully selected students two nights per week. When the dean of the program offered me the job, immediately I thought: "I'll have more time to do research and more time with the family." So I jumped at the chance.

This one course, which ran for a full year, was designed to cover all the humanities subjects required by the core curriculum: Classics, Comparative Literature, English Composition, History, and Philosophy. The students were all unusually bright and successful at their jobs — some in business, others in the arts, and a few in public service administration.

During my first year teaching the course, all the students were able to master the material and to complete their heavy reading and writing assignments, mostly by working like mad on the weekends. My second year also was going well until the second semester, when two students did poorly on the midterm examination and then plagiarized their major research papers. Of course these papers received failing grades and, as the college required, I had to report their plagiarism to the dean. The students, both of whose husbands were prominent alumni and fundraisers of the college, complained to him that I was treating them unfairly. They gathered a few other struggling students to join them in his office for their protest. He apparently assured them he would take care of everything. When another larger group of the more mature and successful students heard about what the others were doing, they also went to see the dean or wrote him letters to support me. Apparently, however, these mattered little because he was so afraid that his program, which he often boasted about as the best in the college, would have its reputation tarnished and he would be embarrassed.

The dean finally called me to his office and asked me to show him the evidence of cheating. Luckily I had photocopies of the papers. He had to agree that both students copied their entire research papers from various published sources and presented these as their own work. He asked, "Are you going to fail them for the course?" I replied, "I'm not sure. They will have to get solid A grades on their final exams to make up for the F grades on the papers." He looked very worried and then said, "But we never fail students in this program, so you have to do something." After thinking for a while, he continued, "I'll tell you what to do: You must disregard these papers and give each of them a chance to write another paper." I was quite upset and blurted out, "But that's not honest! It's not professional. I couldn't do such a thing — I'd never sleep at night!" He got more upset than I was and warned: "If you don't do what I say, you can no longer teach in my program!" I just turned around and walked out without another word.

Two other teachers, close acquaintances of mine, taught the other two sections of the course, so I rushed off to ask them to go back to the dean with me so we could show a united front. When I explained what happened, the older one, a highly respected teacher and full professor, listened patiently and then said: "Well, he's the dean and I can't tell him what to do." And the second one, who was an associate professor and also older than I was, said quite bluntly: "I don't want to get involved. I can't jeopardize my own job in the program." I was shocked. I thought they were my friends. I'd been to their homes and knew their families and they knew mine. I was beginning to feel quite abandoned.

Finally I went to the chair of the English department where I felt sure I would get some support. He was a politically savvy administrator who knew a lot about how the college worked. He also knew my dean. All he could say was that he agreed with me that plagiarism is the chief academic sin and that students must be held accountable, but then he threw his hands in the air and admitted: "The dean has much influence around here and I don't see how I can do anything." This devastated me. I felt betrayed by all those I was sure would help me. Over and over I said to myself: "No one seems to care about honesty anymore! I'm all alone!"

When I went to my next class, I was told that it was being taught by another teacher. That's how I found out I was really fired. All the best students in the class wrote blistering letters to the dean and sent copies to me. At least *they* were kind and supportive. Also my chair assured me I could resume teaching next term in the English department. But for the rest of the term I had no teaching duties. It was a very dark time and I could not understand why God was allowing this to happen. Where was the Providence I had felt so often before?

*   *   *   *   *   *

Left with a mystery

At times like these we might well feel that Providence fails to help us. No matter how much we hope and how hard we pray, nothing seems to be happening and we never are able to understand why. We are left with a mystery.

God seems to be helping us most of the time, but once in a while he seems to hide and leave us on our own. We feel disappointment or failure, and have little or no hope. We have to simply grit our teeth and bear it.

Jesus gave us an example of what to do when there is no light and no hope. At the most terrible moment of his life, when he was hanging on the cross, he cried out to his Father: "Why have you forsaken me?" And he got no answer. He was left with the mystery. He did more than grit his teeth and bear it, however; he made a profound act of love and trust in his Father: "Into your hands I commend my spirit."

In our dark moments, we too have to hang onto our faith in Divine Providence and even in such moments try to seek the kingdom of God. At such times we have to say to ourselves, to remind ourselves of what we know: "God loves us immensely."

Reflections

It is most difficult to escape the black moods that come when things don't happen the way we want them to, when they cause suffering for us and for those we love. Perhaps we have even gotten angry with God and told him — in effect — that he does not know how to use his Providence as he should.

Tom, for instance, felt bad for a long time after he was fired from his cushy teaching job. Mary had to remind him several times that once he was free from that job and returned to work for the college as a whole, many good things happened to him. "Look at all the creative things you were able to do!" she said. "You helped start a very popular religious studies program and invented and taught several new religion courses. With the administration's financial support, you took intensive courses in Islam and studied Judaism and the Bible to prepare to teach your course in the Religions of the West."

Mary was right. After being fired, Tom was set free to do many other things: to join the provost when she asked him to help establish a radically new core curriculum and to chair the faculty development seminars held in the summers to help teachers understand and implement their core vision by working as a team. He was also free to chair the federally funded visitors' program that the faculty used to spread their ideas to over a hundred other colleges by bringing administrators to the campus for three-day programs.

"It was because of all this work," Mary reminded Tom, "that you were more quickly promoted to associate professor and full professor, which brought raises in your salary that helped our large family survive. Maybe none of this would have happened if you didn't get out of that cushy job."

Looking at the big picture, then, Tom had to admit that getting fired turned out to be one of the best things that could have happened.

We are both convinced that God's Providence never does what we want it to when we get preoccupied with our downfalls and look at them by themselves and out of context. God never neglects the larger context; he always sees the whole picture. Being aware of these elements in God's Providence has brought us great consolation.

Questions

1. How might Divine Providence have been at work in the dark moments of your life?
2. When have you blamed God for what happened in your life?
3. What makes it hard to forgive those who wronged you?
4. Why is it difficult to leave the past behind and live fully in the present?

Final Thoughts

These little episodes from the life of our family might suggest the false idea that we have lived a charmed life, a fairy-tale existence in which everything always has a happy ending. It may seem as if the Goddess Fortuna has favored us too much, making sure that on her wheel of fortune our family always ended up on top. Or in more modern terms, it might seem that we are simply lucky guys who have had a pretty easy life.

To some extent that is true, for we have experienced what Julian of Norwich repeated over and over: "All will be well, all will be well!" Like little children, we believe that we have a father who loves us much more than we love each other — even much more than each of us loves himself or herself — and who can do anything.

This faith gives us an optimism that seems to overcome every suffering. This faith helps us to see beyond the surface of things and to be aware of the divine in everything. This faith gives meaning to whatever we do and to whatever happens to us. It makes us see, and gives us the peace that Julian had — "All will be well."

We have to admit that we are fortunate. We have faith that God loves us immensely and are convinced that every event in our lives somehow demonstrates that divine love. We don't always see it, but we believe that it is always there. And as this book demonstrates over and over, God has intervened in our lives so often with concrete acts of loving kindness — his Providence, his love for us — that we not only believe but *know* that God is Love.

Further Reading

Publications from New City Press, Hyde Park, New York:

Gold, Lorna. *New Financial Horizons: the Emergence of an Economy of Communion* (2010).

James, Michael, et al. *Education's Highest Aim: Teaching and Learning through the Spirituality of Communion* (2010).

Living City, the Focolare monthly magazine.

Lubich, Chiara. *Essential Writings: Spirituality, Dialogue, Culture* (2007).

Masters, Thomas and Amy Uelmen. *Focolare: Living the Spirituality of Unity in the United States* (2011).

Websites

Adoption at a distance: www.famiglienuove.org/sostegnoadistanza.php (English translation available)

Economy of Communion: http://www.edc-online.org/en.html

Living City: http://www.livingcitymagazine.com/

New City Press: http://www.newcitypress.com/

New Humanity Movement: http://www.focolare.org/en/movimento-dei-focolari/un-popolo/umanita-nuova/

Acknowledgements

We want to thank all those who have helped us learn how to live a fuller family life: our parents, our sisters and brothers, our children, and our many friends.

We owe a special thanks to those who helped us realize the spiritual dimensions of family living: Chiara Lubich for her inspiring life and her prolific publications, particularly about divine providence and the art of loving; Igino Giordani (Foco) for his many insights into and his example of holiness in the family; Annamaria and Danilo Zanzucchi for their wisdom and model of family living and their personal kindness to us.

For their encouragement in helping us live a gospel-centered life, and for their supporting our attempts to help others, we thank Sharry Silvi, Nuzzo Grimaldi, Julian Ciabattini, and especially Marigen Lohla and Terry Gunn, who were most helpful while we were writing this book.

To Gary Brandl and his staff at New City Press we are most grateful. We want to acknowledge the enormous help that Tom Masters gave us, especially for his innumerable suggestions for improving the text. Other fine suggestions were made by Tommy Hartmann, Julie James, Christina Matone, and Nancy O'Donnell. And special thanks to Durva Correia for designing the cover. Working together with this team was never a burden but always a joy.

About the Authors

Mary is a registered nurse and a holistic health educator. She has worked with families for over twenty years in schools for children with special needs. Tom is Professor Emeritus of English and Religion at Brooklyn College, CUNY, where he worked for over forty years. He is also an editor for New City Press and *Living City* magazine. In addition to their professional work, they were responsible for the New Families Movement for eighteen years in Canada and the United States. They have been married for over forty years and have ten children and twenty grandchildren.